# Social Sciences and Humanities in North East India (1947-97)

J.P. Singh
R. Gopalakrishnan
L.S. Gassah
D.R. Syiemlieh
C.J. Thomas

2026
Regency Publications
*A Division of*
Astral International Pvt. Ltd.
New Delhi – 110 002

*First Published, 1998*

*Reprinted, 2026*

ISBN: 978-81-86030-79-0 (Hardback)



*Published by* : **Regency Publications**
*A Division of*
**Astral International Pvt. Ltd.**
– ISO 9001:2015 Certified Company –
4736/23, Ansari Road, Darya Ganj
New Delhi-110 002
Ph. 011-43549197, 23278134
E-mail: info@astralint.com
Website: www.astralint.com

*Printed at* : **Replika Press Pvt. Ltd.**

भारतीय सामाजिक विज्ञान अनुसंधान परिषद
पूर्वोत्तर क्षेत्रीय केन्द्र
INDIAN COUNCIL OF SOCIAL SCIENCE RESEARCH
NORTH EASTERN REGIONAL CENTRE
NEHU Campus, Shillong - 793022

ICSSR - NERC

Phone : 0364 - 2550436 (O)
0364 - 2550431 (O)
Fax : 0364 - 2550428
e-mail : icssr_nerc@hotmail.com
website : www.icssrnerc.org

# FOREWORD

**Prof. Bhagirathi Panda**
**Honorary Director.**

9th August 2024

The North Eastern Regional Centre (NERC) of the Indian Council of Social Science Research (ICSSR) stands as a pivotal institution, encapsulating the essence of scholarly pursuit and social transformation within the unique cultural tapestry of India's northeastern region. Established in consonance with the broader vision of the ICSSR, NERC serves as a vibrant hub for interdisciplinary research, academic collaboration, and policy discourse, tailored specifically to address the multifaceted socio-economic, political, and cultural dynamics prevalent in the northeastern states. NERC embodies the commitment of the Indian Council of Social Science Research to decentralize research activities and promote inclusivity in the academic landscape. Since its inception, NERC has emerged as a beacon of intellectual inquiry, fostering an ecosystem conducive to the exploration of regional issues while maintaining a global perspective. Its geographical focus extends across the eight states of Arunachal Pradesh, Assam, Manipur, Meghalaya, Mizoram, Nagaland, Tripura, and Sikkim, encompassing a diverse array of ethnicities, languages, and socio-political complexities.

The period between 1947 and 1997 marked significant developments in the social sciences and humanities in North-East India, a region characterized by its rich cultural diversity and unique socio-political landscape. Several trends emerged during this time span, reflecting both the challenges and opportunities faced by the region. This book focuses on trends in social sciences and humanities in North East India, which play a crucial role in advancing knowledge, informing policy, preserving culture, building capacity, and fostering community engagement. They serve as a catalyst for inclusive and sustainable development in the region. The trends in social sciences and humanities in North East India hold immense importance as they facilitate knowledge generation, academic collaboration, and evidence-based policymaking. By critically examining the socio-cultural dynamics of the region, fostering interdisciplinary dialogue, and promoting inclusive approaches, these proceedings contribute to fostering a deeper understanding of North East India's complexities and pave the way for positive social change and sustainable development. The collection of essays in the book should be updated in another collection of essays and include other areas of study.

I am confident that this work will provide readers with a thorough understanding of the extensive research conducted in North East India over the past 50 years. Encompassing disciplines such as economics, folklore, geography, history, philosophy, political science, sociology, and language studies including Assamese, Garo, and English, the volume offers insights both within and beyond the region. Additionally, by including papers on health, contemporary issues in the north-east, and journalism, the compilation establishes connections to the present state of affairs in the area.

I hope that this book will serve as a valuable resource for researchers, educators and policymakers interested in the region. The diverse perspectives and cutting-edge research presented in this book will contribute to the advancement of sustainable practices and professional development, and inspire future generations to continue the quest for a better world. Congratulations to all the contributors and editors for their hard work and dedication in putting this remarkable publication.

Bhagirathi Panda

# Preface

The Screening Committee of the NERC-ICSSR decided to hold a one day seminar as part of the celebration of the 50th year of India's Independence. It was also decided to hold the seminar on the topic Trends in Social Sciences and Humanities in North East India (1947–97). For certain reasons later, contemporary North East, Health and Journalism were also included. The present volume includes the papers presented at the seminar. Several scholars invited to contribute papers to the seminar and participate in the deliberations declined the offer. Many others accepted our invitation but later expressed their inability to present their papers and participate in the seminar. There were others however, who readily accepted our invitation and kept their word. We thank them all for their cooperation.

Altogether twelve articles were submitted, out of these only eleven could be presented in three sessions. The twelfth paper was taken as read due to shortage of time. The seminar was organised in three sessions — The Inaugural Session, and the First and Second Academic Sessions.

The Inaugural Session of the Seminar was held in the Mayurbhanj Seminar Hall on 30th March 1998 at 10.00 A.M., and was presided over by Professor Milton Sangma, Pro-Vice Chancellor, NEHU Campus, Tura, and was inaugurated by Shri M.M. Jacob, the Hon'ble Governor of Meghalaya.

The Inaugural Session began with the Welcome address. Professor J.P. Singh, Honorary Director, NERC-ICSSR welcomed Shri M.M. Jacob, the Hon'ble Governor of Meghalaya, Professor B. Pakem, Vice-Chancellor, NEHU, Professor Milton Sangma, the participants, colleagues and students and all the others. Thereafter, Shri M.M. Jacob, the Governor of Meghalaya delivered his inaugural address. The inaugural address was followed by the First paper of the Seminar by Professor B. Pakem on Trends in Political Science in North East India. The Seminar Hall was full to the capacity. Professor Milton Sangma then gave his Presidential remarks. Professor L.S. Gassah then proposed a vote of thanks to all.

The inaugural session was followed by the First Academic Session at 11.30 A.M. It was presided over by Professor J.P. Singh, Honorary Director, ICSSR-NEHU and altogether six papers were presented by 1) Shri Wasbir Hussain, 2) Professor A.C. Mohapatra, 3) Dr. D.R. Syiemlieh 4) Dr. N. Srivastav 5) Dr. H. Ghonglah and 6) Professor Milton S. Sangma. The session was over by 1.45 P.M.

The Second Academic Session started at 2.15 P.M. after lunch. It was again presided over by Professor Milton S. Sangma. In this session also six papers were presented by 1) Dr. Soumen Sen, 2) Dr. S. C. Daniel, 3) Dr. Nikhlesh Kumar, 4) Dr A.S. Guhu and 5) Dr B.K. Deb Sarma. The next sixth paper of Shri Sanat Chakravarty was taken as read. Professor Sangma at the end gave his remarks, and asked Dr. Joshua Thomas to propose a vote of thanks.

Papers presented in both the sessions of the seminar were liked by all those who participated in the deliberations. Several participants asked searching questions and some of them also gave their own comments on the papers presented. The general response of the participants and their interaction indicated their appreciation of the papers presented.

The papers presented at the seminar, (in some cases) were revised subsequently.

Subsequently, these papers were revised and arranged in the same order, as they were presented at the Seminar. This was done, in order to retain thematic continuity.

Inspite of all our efforts it is possible that many mistakes of ommission and commission may have crept in this publication. We crave the indulgence of the reader for the same.

**Editors**

# Contents

# List of Contributors

**Shri M.M. Jacob**
Governor of Meghalaya
Shillong

**Professor B. Pakem**
Vice Chancellor
NEHU/Shillong

**Professor A.C. Mohapatra**
Dean
School of Human & Environmental Sciences
NEHU/Shillong

**Dr. D.R. Syiemlieh**
Department of History
NEHU/Shillong

**Dr. N. Srivastav**
Department of Economics
NEHU/Shillong

**Dr. Soumen Sen**
Centre For Literary & Cultural Studies
NEHU/Shillong

**Dr. S.C. Daniel**
Department of Philosophy
NEHU/Shillong

**Dr. Nikhlesh Kumar**
Department of Sociology
NEHU/Shillong

**Professor Milton Sangma**
Pro-Vice Chancellor
NEHU Tura Campus

**Dr. B.K. Dev Sarma**
Director
College Development Council
NEHU/Shillong

**Dr. A.S. Guha**
Regional Director
IGNOU/Shillong

**Shri Wasbir Hussain**
Special Correspondent
The Asian Age
Guwahati

**Shri Sanat Chakraborty**
Editor
Grass Roots Options

**Dr. H. Ghonglah**
Directorate of Health Services
Government of Meghalaya
Shillong

# Inaugural Address

*Shri M.M. Jacob*
*Governor of Meghalaya*

I deem it a great honour and a privilege to be invited to inaugurate today's seminar on "Trends in Social Sciences in North East India 1947–97" organised by the Indian Council of Social Science Research, North Eastern Regional Centre. I am grateful to the Chairman of the Indian Council of Social Science Research, all its office-bearers and other members of the Council for giving me this opportunity.

The geography and the history of the North-Eastern Region have created a very distinctive socio-economic, cultural and political milieu. The socio-economic and political setting of the North-Eastern Region has direct linkages with the order where the tribal form of society and economy occupy the vantage position. The order that exists today has ramifications of the three-fold division of societies into tribal, traditional and modern ones to which have been associated different forms of economy. The topography, geology and the general natural setting of the region have endowed it with considerable natural resources — fertile soil, lush forests, fossil fuels, minerals and abundant water potential. The economic activities and growth impulses in the region find their base in these natural resources.

The geographic structure of the region, criss-crossed by numerous lines of hills and endless streams and rivers, made communication to and within this region immensely difficult.

The geographical isolation, coupled with a series of socio-political and historical obstacles, kept this region out of the caravan of national progress. When freedom of India dawned, the people of this region were found to be educationally backward, economically handicapped, socially confused and politically frustrated. However, the rapid expansion in the field of education which took place in the wake of India's Independence, exposed the people of this region to new ideas. When educational advancement came, a new consciousness for political identity arose and a new urge also was evident for early fulfilment of socio-economic aspirations.

The British first established their rule in the Brahmaputra Valley after the signing of the famous Treaty of Yandobo between the British and the Burmese on the 24th February, 1826. The British Government adopted a policy of keeping the tribal areas isolated from the rest of the country. The Government of India Act 1935, provided for delimitation of Excluded and Partially Excluded Areas, which were partly under the direct administrative control of the Governor. The dealings of the British with the hill areas of the then State of Assam underwent a change dictated by exigencies. This led to the introduction of the Inner Line Regulation of 1873 in certain areas of North East India.

The region under the British regime witnessed changes in all spheres of life. There was an expansion of activities of the missionaries in the spread of education, Christianity, health services etc. There were also far reaching effects in the field of economy of the region and its communication network. However, the British policy of 'Divide and Rule' led to gradual contempt and distrust for imperialism. A host of political leaders from this region took part in the freedom struggle led by Gandhiji.

Historically, the areas in the North-Eastern Region came under the British rule much later than the other parts of the country. The dualistic composition of the population — ethnically, the tribals and the non-tribals and geographically, the hill people and the plains people — is nowhere so well-marked as in the North Eastern Region. After Independence, the government's tribal policy, though not expressly stated as such, appeared to aim at overcoming the problems created by long neglect and indifference of the Raj towards the tribal people. Jawaharlal Nehru, the main architect of government's tribal policy in the immediate post-Independence period, was in favour of going slow in the matter of inducing changes in the tribal areas. "Above all" he wrote "I hope there will be no attempt made to impose other ways of life on them in a hurry. Let the changes come gradually, and be worked out by the tribals themselves."

Initially, all the areas of the region, excepting Manipur and Tripura, were within the then State of Assam. Arunachal Pradesh, then known as NEFA, had a separate arrangement; it was kept as an Agency, to be administered and developed under the special care of the Centre. Some autonomy in the form of the Autonomous District Councils was provided under the Sixth Schedule to the Constitution for administrative convenience. However, with the passage of time, a number of causes led to several demands for separate Statehood within and even outside the Indian federal set-up. These developments led to the emergence of Nagaland as a State in 1963, and subsequently, of Meghalaya, Manipur and Tripura as full-fledged States and Arunachal Pradesh and Mizoram as Union Territories in 1972. The region continued with this set up for a long time until 1987, when both Arunachal Pradesh and Mizoram were declared as States of the Indian Union. The North Eastern Council (NEC) was also set up under an Act of Parliament in 1972 as an advisory body and to serve as a common platform for all the seven States where they can come together to discuss common problems involving more than one State or all of them.

The North-East, which comprises 8 per cent of India's total area and just 4 per cent of its total population is nature's paradise. Its hills and valleys have witnessed centuries of migration. It was a gateway of commerce and culture that linked India with the East and South East Asia.

Looking back on the 50 years of Independence I think the North-Eastern region has grown and progressed with the rest of India, though many gaps remain still. I would say that we need to concentrate on the strengths of this region which are:

— High literacy rate as compared to that of some other States of the country.

— Tremendous hydro-electric potential.
— Proximity of South-East India.
— High percentage of untapped mineral wealth.
— The fertile areas available in the plains, capable of feeding the entire region if properly utilised.

Today, we live in a globally inter-connected world, in which biological, psychological, social and environmental phenomena are interdependent. We need an ecological perspective, a holistic approach, which the earlier 19th century did not provide. It would be indeed a new paradigm, a new vision of reality. India's North-East is not an island. It is linked culturally and politically with other parts of India. Much has been written and spoken about mistakes leading to problems in the region. We should learn from past mistakes. We must view the positive and negative developments that have taken place during the past five decades in this region with scientific detachment and come to rational conclusions. I am sure this seminar will be a major step in this direction.

With these words I have great pleasure in inaugurating the seminar on "Trends in Social Sciences in North East India 1947–97" and wish the deliberations all success.

Jai Hind,
Khublei,
Mithela.

# 1

# Trends in Political Science Studies in North-East India, 1947–1997

*B. Pakem*

---

The study of Political Science is one of the important areas of study for the under-graduate and post-graduate studies among the arts students of North-East India ever since 1947. Till that year the colleges of North-East India were affiliated to the Calcutta University. It was only in 1948 that the first University in the region was established in Guwahati. However, the study of Political Science was only a part of the course in the Department of Economics both at the under-graduate and post-graduate levels. A separate Department of Political Science was established only during 1959-60. The establishment of other Universities of Dibrugarh (1966); North-Eastern Hill University (1973); Manipur (1980); Arunachal (1985); Tripura (1987); Assam (1994); and Nagaland (1994) also include courses in Political Science Studies.[1]

So, during the period of Fifty Years after India's Independence we can see the rapid progress in the study of this important academic discipline. In fact, the majority of students in North-East India have always opted for this course both at the under-graduate and post-graduate levels. Inspite of the ever increasing number of degree holders in Political Science and the saturation point has been reached during the last fifty years, the trend continues to be in the upward swing.

So far nobody has made any serious attempt to analyse this extra-ordinary trend in Political Science Studies, excepting for a general statement that (a) Political Science is an easy course for general students, and (b) a study of politics is both exciting and exhilarating. But this is only an over-simplification of the true status of Political Science Studies, since a number of students in competitive civil service examinations would opt for some other courses which are more scoring than in Political Science. The reason must lie somewhere else.

The fact is that Political Science as a separate academic discipline is flourishing only by mid 60s and new departments of Political Science in the colleges started coming up around that time. There is, therefore, ample opportunities for students of Political Science to gain employment in the ever growing number of colleges offering course of studies in Political Science. True by 1986 the requisite qualifications of 55% alongwith National Eligibility Test Certificates have to a certain extent affected student of Political Science to gain entry into the college and university teaching posts. However, unlike disciplines like Anthropology and Sociology, students of Political Science can still enter the job market at the Higher Secondary School level apart from jobs in the public sector. Now that the rate of educated unemployed Political Scientists is gradually rising, the trend may undergo a change after 50 years of fruitful experience in the field of Political Science Studies.

From the under-graduate and post-graduate studies in political science we may pass on to the field of research in the discipline. The trend in this area of study is somewhat halting and slow in the beginning. It was only during 1969-70 that there were four doctorate degree holders in political science under the Gauhati University — D.P. Barua on Indo-British Relations 1950–60; L.C. Singh on British Relations with Manipur 1824–1891; M.N. Borgohain on the Assam Legislative Assembly 1937–67; and S.K. Barpujari on Anglo-Naga Relations.[2]

If we add Public Administration which was then a part of Political Science then we have another doctorate degree in Political Science during the same period — N.I. Singh on The Manipur Administration 1709–1907.[3] As a matter of fact, the first Ph.D. in Political Science was U.N. Bordoloi on Local Finance in Assam who was awarded the degree in 1967 but listed under the discipline of Economics.[4] By the same token another Ph.D. in Political Science in 1977 was P.S. Reddi on

The Working of the Sixth Schedule in North-East India though he was listed under the discipline of Law.[5] Thus, there is no detailed account of Political Science research under one list. We have to do a little more exercise in searching for the total output of research works in the discipline of Political Science over the last 50 years.

The other new Universities started opening their innings late in the 70s. Dibrugarh University produced a first Ph.D. in Political Science in 1972— B. Pakem on India-Burma Ralations;[6] and the North-Eastern Hill University in 1983 — D. Bhattacharjee on Higher Bureaucracy in Meghalaya and its role in Development.[7] I have yet to lay my hands on the list of research work in Political Science in the other Universities in the region. Perhaps the list of 100 Ph.D. degree holders under the supervisorship of Prof. V. Venkata Rao would indicate the true trends in the field of research in Political Science in North-East India ranging from local Government to Public Administration, history, foreign relations and government and politics.[8] This is still the trend today even after 50 years of Political Science Research in North-East India not only in the colleges and Universities but also among the non-governmental research agencies in Social Sciences.

In the 80s the universities in North-East India had also started courses for M.Phil students in Political Science. The main thrust of the M.Phil courses in these universities is on Research Methodology preparing research students for further research in Political Science in a more scientific way. Since there is not enough literature in the field of studies for M.Phil. degrees it is somewhat difficult to properly assess the trend in M.Phil. research programme. But from my experience in the M.Phil. programmes of the Department of Political Science of the North-Eastern Hill University and as an evaluator of M.Phil. dissertations of some universities in the region it indicates that the trend in M.Phil. studies in Political Science is more towards understanding the local issues and less on other issues like foreign relations, political theory and law.

Another aspect of the M.Phil. courses in the Universities of the region is that the importance of the M.Phil. degree in Political Science is being devalued in the sense that some universities would offer a direct Ph.D. course in Political Science rather than the M.Phil course. Even students would prefer to do a direct Ph.D. course instead of spending about two years for the M.Phil degree, thus reducing the number of years for completing their Ph.D. Programmes. In some universities like the North-Eastern Hill University, the M.Phil course which was compulsory during the 80s and early 90s has now become optional. The M.Phil course which is a good preparatory ground for sound research pursuit in later years of the scholars has of late attracted mainly the teachers who would like to earn an M.Phil degree as a faculty improvement programme for their career advancement. It is an alarming trend indeed which may require a serious attention by political scientists of the region, more particularly on the "pronounced weakness" of M.Phil syllabi.[9]

The next point to be discussed in this paper is on the course content of Political Science Studies in North-East India during the last 50 years or so. The *Survey of Research in Political Science* conducted by the Indian Council for Social Science Research has dealt with the Five main fields of Political Science Studies in five volumes on Political System, Political Process, Political Dynamics, Political Thought and International Studies.[10] A cursory glance over the courses, and research programmes in Political Science in the Colleges and Universities of North-East India indicates that the trend in North-East India is on the study of the first two and the last two groups while the study of Political Dynamics takes a back seat. This is true at all levels of studies — undergraduate, post-graduate, and research programmes in Political Science. True, of late, Political Dynamics is also gaining ground indicating thereby a promising trend in modern Political Science studies in North-East India.

Similarly, the same courses of Political Science Studies and research programmes in the region fall more or less along with the five main divisions of the courses of studies as pointed out by the *Curriculum Development Centre in Political Science* sponsored by the University Grants Commission. These five divisions cover the fields of studies in Political Theory and Research Methodology; Public Administration; International Relations; Indian Government and Politics; and Comparative Politics.[11]

The Universities in the region are offering two kinds of courses for the post-graduate students — the conventional two years' eight-paper course and the sixteen-paper course of four semesters' duration of six months each. Both the courses, however, have a number of optional courses for almost all the above five divisions. In the North-Eastern Hill University which adopts the semester system has a provision for an internal assessment as well. In the 70s and early 80s the internal assessment was of 50 per cent weightage which has been later on reduced to 25 per cent only. There was, however, a line of thinking in NEHU during the mid-90s to do away with the system of internal assessment, citing among other reasons the question of the system being less objective. It only indicates about the trend in the discipline of Political Science in the region leading towards more objectivity in studies and research.

In this connection, it is perhaps worthwhile to ponder over what the Curriculum Development Centre in Political Science had observed in connection with the optional courses and the semester courses. In the case of optionals it was observed that there has been a "draw back" of "the vast array of options offered" which in fact is "merely a paper exercise".[12] This is true in the case of the Universities in the region for no fault of theirs. The implementation of any ambitious scheme for a wider range of optional courses would require adequate infrastructural facilities like the lecture halls, library books and periodicals. It also requires a sufficient number of faculty members to properly handle the optional papers. But the Universities in North-East India are not well equipped with these requirements due to financial constraints.

Similarly, the semester system has not been well received by the Curriculum Development Centre in Political Science. The Centre has observed that; "An eight-paper work-load cannot be transmitted into an (apparently) sixteen-paper work-load without damage to quality and comprehensiveness of the instruction imparted."[13] Inspite of this observation, Universities, like NEHU, still follow the semester system in view of the fact that a continuous assessment of the students is expected to produce a better result. The contention of NEHU seems to be justifiable in view of the fact that its Political Science students can successfully compete in the national level examinations and tests. This can be verified from the statements issued by the University Grants Commission from time to time.

Another discernible trend in Political Science Studies in North-East India is the special thrust area given to the study and research of regional issues, problems and prospectives. But, this is perhaps true of every University in the country. The only difference is that the emphasis in Political Science Studies in North-East India on indigenous studies and research is on a priority basis rather than of a perfunctorily character as in the Universities outside the region. This trend is perhaps due to the exceptional political situations prevailing in the region. In fact even in some Universities outside the region, as in the Calcutta University, we have a strong centre of North-Eastern India study in the Department of Political Science for similar reasons. While this may become a healthy trend in knowing more about one's own area, yet there is a danger in such a trend which may lead to studies and research in political science being isolated from the universal trend towards an integrated programme of study and research in the discipline. I fully subscribe to the observation made by the Curriculum Development Centre: "A carefully elicited curriculum necessarily had to reflect and stress indigenous needs; but a study of these could prove sterile unless they were anchored to, and a reflection of, universal referents, and made their own, creatively indigenous contribution to the latter."[14]

It may also be noted here that in the course of the last 50 years of political science studies and research in the region, the discipline tends to become unwieldy in the sense that more often than not it has to cross over into the fields of study and research pertaining to other disciplines. But this trend is taking place in the rest of the country too. These days, we usually hear more and more about the need to have an inter-disciplinary study covering not only other social science disciplines like Political History and Political Sociology but also in the other inter-related science streams, like Political Geography, Political Anthropology and Political Philosophy. While in the rest of the country, particularly in the cosmopolitan universities, inter-disciplinary studies and research have become almost a modern academic fashion, the universities in North-East India offering Political Science courses are by and large still traditional in outlook and have yet to fully join the mainstream of modern intellectual fashion. But does it really matter much? True in the West, political scientists have a more rigorous intellectual exercise in inter-disciplinary studies and research. In India, however, the Curriculum Development Centre has rightly cautioned the political scientists that inter-disciplinary studies and research in Political Science may "degenerate into the sterile, unfocussed multi-disciplinary (or cross-disciplinarity) of an a-disciplinary (or counter-disciplinary) sort", and "inter-disciplinary studies in India were often little more than descriptive, information-trotting exercises."[15]

This caution may be a very sound one indeed. But in North-East India we have not yet reached even the threshold of this caution. The trend in North-East India lies somewhere else. Before North-East Indian Political Scientists could further delve into the intricacies of inter-disciplinary, multi-disciplinary, a-disciplinary or counter-disciplinary studies and research, the mere vastness of the size and extent of the current status of political science discipline makes it necessary for some of its divisions to claim the status of an autonomous discipline. Public Administration is quite illustrative. The trend today in the Universities of the region, like NEHU, is to have a separate discipline/department of Public Administration. The next trend in autonomy development in the region, say, by the beginning of the third millenium, would be the autonomous status for International Relations. Ultimately, we as political scientists of the region, may have to be contented with the core content of the discipline of Political Science — Political Theory, Government and Politics.

When we talk about the trends in Political Science studies and research in North-East India, we cannot also ignore the emerging trend regarding the problem of regional language concerning translation, writing, and publication of text books. This is a particular problem for the Brahmaputra Valley. But the trend is gradually spreading to other areas starting with the regional language components of reading materials in Political Science studies at the higher secondary school level. Even in the hill areas of the region where English has been the language for the study and research in Political Science, many find it necessary to take recourse to local language in the absence of a regional language. In narrating all this, it is not my intention to question the decision of the authorities concerned for switching over to a regional language. There is nothing wrong in having a regional language for the purpose of study and research in Political Science. It would have been a more welcoming trend provided the quality of regional language text books in the discipline would be at par with the English, French or German text books. As late as 1991, the finding of the Curriculum Development Centre is that there is a "woeful dearth of reading materials of even reasonable quality in the regional languages."[16] This, to a certain extent, is also true in the case of North-East India situation. Unless the concerned authorities pay their serious attention to the need producing adequate teaching and reading materials in regional languages, it would be an alarming trend in political science study and research. It would be an alarming trend in the sense that the political scientists of the region may be deprived of the sources of knowledge in the discipline that may be otherwise available in each other language groups. There are definitely better sources of knowledge in Assamese or Bengali languages which political scientists from the hill areas of the region may be deprived of and vice-versa.

In view of the fact that today political science covers a vast field of knowledge. It is very necessary that political scientists of North-East India should keep abreast with the latest development in the ever growing literature of this "master science". Because of its vastness, it is also imperative on the part of the political scientists of the region not to remain contented with its general aspect alone. We should also appreciate the specialised aspect of the discipline. This has to be emphasised because in North-East India, the current trend is, for a majority of political scientists, to have only a general study of their discipline and very few of them would go for a particular specialisation. I am only indicating the trend rather than entering into a debate on the issue between the generalists verus the specialists. However, for those who are entering the teaching profession in political science, it would be advisable that they should have specialised at least in one field of the discipline particularly at the post-graduate and research levels. I hope that this trend may also reflect itself at the collegiate level during the next fifty years of political science studies and research in North-East India.

## REFERENCES

1. *Universities Hand-Book*, Association of Indian Universities, New Delhi, 27th Edition, December 1997.
2. *A Bibliography of Doctoral Dissertations Accepted by Indian Universities, 1857–1970*, (Inter-University Board of India, New Delhi, 1974), Section II; pp. 33, 37; Entry Nos. 296, 297, 301, 332.
3. Ibid., p. 62, Entry No. 549.
4. Ibid., Section III, p. 72, Entry No. 658, see also Pakem, B., "A Survey of Social Science Research Works conducted in Shillong", in Pakem, B., *Shillong 1971–81*, (Research India Publications, Calcutta, 1984) For North-East India Council for Social Science Research, Shillong, p. 156.
5. Ibid., 1976-77 (New Delhi, 1979), *Social Science and Humanities*, p. 27, Entry, No. 179.
6. Ibid., 1970–75 (New Delhi, 1979), *Social Science and Humanities*, p. 49, Entry, No. 402.
7. Ibid., 1982-83 (New Delhi, 1986), *Social Science and Humanities*, p. 41, Entry, No. 280.
8. Sangma, M.S. (Ed.), *Essays on North-East India*, (Indian Publishing Company, New Delhi, 1994), Appendix B.
9. *Report of the Curriculum Development Centre in Political Science*, (University Grants Commission, New Delhi, 1991), p. 180.
10. Indian Council of Social Science Research, *Survey of Research in Political Science*, (Allied Publishers, 1979).
11. F.N. 9, pp. 12–16.
12. Ibid., p. 179.
13. Ibid.
14. Ibid., p. 187.
15. Ibid., p. 188.
16. Ibid., p. 780.

2

# Northeast India: Half a Century of Teaching and Research in Geography (1947–97)

*A.C. Mohapatra*

## Background

The year of celebrating the Golden Jubilee of India's independence has made it incumbent on all to introspect and assess where we have progressed and where, failed — an opportunity of reorienting ourselves for a journey, perhaps to the next century. So also are, the tasks for the social scientists. A society as diverse and as plural as ours, makes it even an onerous task for the social scientists to guide the nation amidst a maze of obfuscating relationships — political, social and economic.

The emergence of modern Geography in the first quarter of nineteenth century Germany as an academic discipline, taught and researched in universities after the anointing of Karl Ritter in a Chair at the University of Berlin, has been and continues to be between the two horns of the dilemma, whether science (the physical) or the arts (the human)— a controversy that was, and is needless, if the initial agenda of the discipline is grasped — "studying the man-environment relationship", with man as the central focus.

India inherited the British traditions in geography, like many other disciplines following the umbilical cord of academics that linked the inheritance of English education and the British colonisation of India. Geography teaching was introduced in British schools in the middle of the nineteenth century under the advocacy of T.S. Huxley, a natural scientist, geographer, a man of letters and a close friend and follower of Charles Darwin. The objective was quite clear — enhancing the knowledge of the young Britishers about the land and people of the colonies, that catered to efficient management and control of the colonies. The introduction of geography in the University curriculum in Great Britain was a much later affair, promoted not by His Majesty's Government but by the Royal Society dominated by royalties and ex-generals with explicit objectives of explorations and discoveries of new areas and people.[1] Within geography the British tradition remained a weak one until late and thus, its strong influence on the development of a rather weak tradition in India as well.

The genesis of geography education in India followed its introduction in British schools towards the end of the nineteenth century, dominated by regional geography and physical geography. It was shortly followed by introduction in the undergraduate stage, in early part of twentieth century, initially taught by Britishers educated in Britain. The introduction of geography as a University discipline was in early nineteen-thirties at Calcutta University and Aligargh Muslim University. Today geography is taught at the post-graduate level in more than 100 universities and Post-Graduate colleges, churning out about 5000 master degree holders and over a hundred Ph.Ds, annually. The point intended here, is that within this enormous quantitative expansion of teaching and research at the highest level in the Indian university system, *the original agenda was forgotten*, — till late, geography remained largely descriptive, highly fragmented, catering neither to its scientific agenda nor to the social relevance.[2]

## Geographic Teaching and Research in the Northeast India

For the first time, geography teaching and research, at the university level, was introduced in the Northeast region, in early fifties with the establishment of a Post-Graduate department at the Gauhati University (established in 1948, immediately after the Independence). For the next quarter of a century, it remained the sole repository of higher education in geography in the region, till 1976, that a second department came up under the auspices of the North-Eastern Hill University. Currently, there are 8 Post-Graduate departments in Geography in the region, three additions in PG colleges in Assam, (Bajali College, Pathsala, Cotton College, Guwahati and at Jorhat) and in Arunachal University, Manipur University and the Nagaland Central University, in addition to the existing two, at Gauhati University and NEHU. It appears to be a popular subject at the undergraduate level in all the states and remains largely, as part of the social studies at the school level. Currently, around 250 students are enroled for Post-Graduate education in geography in the region. The past three decades have been significant, in the sense that considerable research monographs at the Ph.D. level have been written (over 50)[3], many published but largely remain buried in shelves of university libraries. Research inputs also come by way of publications in reputed journals, books as well as technical reports of research projects[4]. Outlining all of them shall be a daunting task — many of those are not readily accessible. So, the main attempt remains that of being selective coverage that indicate trends in the subject.

## Contributions of Geographic Teaching and Research

The contributions of any academic discipline could be assessed in light of its contributions to the (a) "core problematic", (b) its academic traditions, and (c) the social relevance. The "core problematic" is essentially either the methodological or/ and the core contents of a discipline that distinguishes the discipline from the rest — in Kuhn's sense a paradigm, that allows for a large number of "practitioners" and that tries to answer "significant questions" or raises such questions that other sciences have either neglected or failed to answer.[5] The problem of the "core" was well settled by early German philosophers and geographers.[6] With development of the discipline various academic traditions emerged, in Germany, in the USA, France and in the Great Britain. The social agenda of the discipline though was not absent in the nineteen century geography, particularly, the anarchist school of Kropotkin and Elise Reclus,[7] its impetus has been more in recent times. At another level the assessment must address to contributions in relations to the current research frontiers at one hand, and its contextual foundations, being placed in particular regional, social or "problem context".

As was pointed out earlier, the original agenda of geography that came from the German academics was profoundly biological and anthropogenic view of man and his relationship with the environment.[8] The British geography picked up on a tangent, a deterministic view of geography (as was the early American geography), that attempted to establish the shackles of environment on development of human progress. Truly following this tradition, in general, the geographic research in India churned out treatises, no different from that the former colonial masters, and true to the tradition, the main contributions from the only Post-Graduate department in the region was participating in this much trodden path of the national mainstream. In the past two decades, beginning with the Rhodian Shores,[9] that geography is rediscovering its original agenda, a *biological* and *anthropogenic view.*

Taking the academic tradition into account, one is tempted to refer to the two very first research dissertations in geography, one by Prof. S.P. Chatterjee (1936), *La Plateau de Meghalaya* submitted to University of Paris and of Prof. H.P. Das (1954), *Forest of Assam: A Study in Economic Geography,* submitted to London School of Economics and Political Science.[10] The former used the French traditions of regional geography and the latter, used systematic approach to the study of forests. The tradition is also reflective of the fragmentation of the geographic discourse between the physical and the human, often there having no dialogue between the two.

The question of *social relevance in geography,* i.e., reorienting geographic inquiry to address to the contemporary social and economic issues is of recent origin, roughly three decades old. It emerged partly reacting to the traditional deterministic position and partly revolting against an overtly positivist paradigm, failing to relate to contemporary social discourses.[11] Its echoes found immediate response in India, especially the newly instituted Jawaharlal Nehru University, that broadly tried to influence in changing the directions of research and teaching geography as a principally social science subject and elsewhere, through induction of its products. The social relevance themes in teaching and research in geography in the region was, no doubt introduced by the Department of Geography, NEHU due to its close association with JNU both in research and instruction curriculum. Such changes have now come into research and teaching activities in many departments in the region, though much remains to be done.

## Changes in Focus in Instruction Curriculum

Till the mid-seventies the under-graduate curriculum in geography was dominated by Physical geography, Regional geography of India and world regions, Economic and Human geography, practicals largely dominated by map projection and surveying. This largely remains so even now, except that a variety of optionals (special papers) are visible, like in population geography, cartography, agricultural geography, urban geography and regional planning. There is little improvement in teaching methods and the contents are almost frozen for the past fifty years.

The post-graduate curriculum was no different, except the intensification and the larger number of papers taught till about the mid-seventies. This situation was perhaps, due to either reluctance on part of the teachers to change the syllabus or reluctance to update the courses. This was also due to the inflexibility of the system adopted in curriculum development by various universities. However, with starting of NEHU, some innovations could be discerned, especially the flexibility adopted in curriculum development — revising the syllabus atleast once in three years. This was facilitated by adoption of a semester based curriculum that helped in facilitating in introduction of a large number of new courses, like social geography, historical geography, history and philosophy of geography, regional development and planning, introduction of modern technological inputs in geography in the form of aerial photographs and satellite images and computer applications. Innovations in the form of master's level thesis were also introduced. One could now see that some of these new elements have entered into the post-graduate syllabus of many older and new universities in the region. This is certainly a healthy trend.

## Research

Research contributions could be located in published research monographs and books, technical reports of specific research projects, published literature in professional journals, seminar proceedings, edited volumes and in research programmes in various universities and institutions. These contributions are selectively cited and thematically arranged in major areas of the discipline covered in the region.

Doctoral research programmes in geography was first initiated by the oldest university of the region, the Gauhati University in the mid-fifties. But the actual out-put were far and few between in the initial decades. The numerical expansion in doctoral monographs could be seen from the seventies onwards. However, many of these covered rather traditional areas, like Geomorphology, Population geography, Settlement geography (both rural and urban), Political geography, Agricultural geography etc. Lately, there has been a trend to study new areas like poverty and inequality, ethnic issues — tribes, environmental dimensions etc. A broad classification follows:

### *Environment and Society*

Though environmental concerns remained the traditional focus in geographical research and teaching, little of field based, scientific studies, as such were carried out. There has been a resurgence of interest among geographers in the country to make specific studies on environment in micro and meso regional scales. This finds appropriate echoes in recent studies on environment in the discipline of geography in the region. The studies are both at the level of research programmes as well as on the level of research projects. Konwar (1990) studied Land Classification in West Khasi Hills district of Meghalaya to classify the district into normative classes based on the degree of environmental degradation. Qureshi (1989) studied the agricultural system of the Monpas of Arunachal Pradesh on the basis of their ecological diversities. Baruah (1992) studied the slopes and soil mass movement in Meghalaya.

Technical reports based on specific research studies, like of Mohapatra (1989)[12] dealt with soil erosion and alteration of soil characteristics of West Khasi Hills district of Meghalaya. Another study by Mohapatra et al. (1997)[13] dealt with deforestation and soil erosion in a small watershed of Umran river of Bhoi Area district of Meghalaya. Rai (1997)[14] studied the ecological problems of coal mining areas of Meghalaya.

Professional publications include Mohapatra and Konwar (1993)[15] on land classification in West Khasi Hills district based on aerial photos and satellite images, and also on soil rating classification (1989),[16] Mohapatra (1995)[17] on emerging cycle of poverty and land degradation and responses to the ecological issues, Baruah and Mohapatra (1996)[18] on soil mass movement, Mohapatra (1997)[19] on pricing of urban water supply, Mohapatra (1997)[20] on traditional rights, community participation and forest management in the Northeast and Rai and Agarwal (1993)[21] on geo-environmental hazards around the Umiam reservoir.

## *Geomorphology*

Geomorphology for long has remained one of the major areas of geographical research in the region. Some of these studies do not strictly fall under social science research. These are not taken up here. However, there are others, that are either in the interface of a social science issue or that indirectly addresses to specific social (contextual) problems. A number of such studies are available in form of research monographs (both doctoral and pre-doctoral). A study by Pattanaik (1979) on the relationship of geomorphology and agriculture, Panda (1985), between geomorphology and landuse, Agarwal (1996), on geo-hazards in Umiam river basin and Rinawma's (1987) study of influence of geomorphology on agricultural development in Lunglei district of Mizoram are some such studies to illustrate.[22] This is a welcome approach. There is a need of not only discovering new laws and theories in geomorphology, but also a need to integrate it in aiding actual social (planning) practices, that could make life easier for large sections of people.

*Agricultural Geography*

Agriculture is one of the most studied areas in Indian geography; it is not very different either for the north-east region, as well. Several pre-doctoral, doctoral studies have been carried out over the past two decades, largely on the North-Eastern region, but some on other areas as well. Aziz (1981) worked on agricultural productivity in Mewat, Das (1982) on peasant agriculture in Assam, Datta (1983) on agricultural occupance of Nagaon district of Assam, Sahu (1984) on agricultural diffusion (technology), Chattaraj (1984) on agricultural landuse of Kamrup district, Saikia (1987) on size of holding and productivity in Naogan district, Shukla (1982) on agricultural productivity and planning in Siang, Arunachal Pradesh, Mipun (1987) on agricultural change in lower Brahmaputra Valley and Bhagabati (1990) on spatial analysis of small-scale agriculture of Nalbari district.

No doubt, many of these studies have contributed on "gap filling", generation and compilation of data from primary and secondary sources on agricultural landuse, productivity and other geography specific studies at the state and micro regional levels, but majority of them lack in any fresh theoretical or methodological insights or findings that have direct public policy implications.

Books and research papers published in the field are many. They cover areas of agricultural landuse, size of landholding and tenure system, cropping pattern and intensity, agricultural growth and planning in the region. Barman et al. (1978)[23] studied the crop-combination regions of Assam, Mohapatra (1979)[24] analysed the regional character of Green Revolution, Bhagabati (1984)[25] studied the agricultural productivity in the Brahmaputra Valley, Chattoraj et al. (1983)[26] on intra-district variations in agricultural productivity, Das (1984)[27] analysed the character of peasant agriculture of Assam. Gopalakrishnan (1989)[28] studied the agricultural development in Assam, Goswami (1989),[29] floods and their impact on agriculture in Assam, Rai et al. (1983),[30] the hill slope farming around

Shillong, Shukla (1983),[31] agricultural planning in Arunachal Pradesh, Singh (1977)[32] on irrigation in Manipur and its potentials and Singh (1985)[33] on land capability classification. The subject covered are wide ranging and papers, the most numerous.

### *Geography of Resources, Manufacturing and Marketing*

It is often expounded that the Northeast region is rich in natural resources, but little explored and exploited for the benefits of the people. In areas of resources, manufacturing (Industrial geography including localisation issues) and marketing (and distribution) there are relatively less of doctoral research. Some of the M.Phil./Ph.D. monographs include, Borah (1984) on the tea industry in Assam, Tahbildar (1986) on industrial changes in Jagiroad area, Borah (1988) on energy used for cooking in Guwahati municipal area, Kharkonger (1989) on industrial geography of Meghalaya, Borthakur (1994) on the periodic market system in the region, Pio (1994) on tea economy in lower Brahmaputra valley and Colney (1996) on industrial development of Mizoram with focus on small and cottage industries etc.

Publications in professional journals, edited volumes and books etc in areas of land resources (Bhagabati, 1986;[34] Mohapatra et al., 1982,[35] 1985[36] and 1990[37]; Baruah, 1988[38]), water resources (Goswami, 1992[39]), power resources (Mohapatra, 1992[40]), Mineral resources (Chandra, 1984[41]), Forest resources (Das, 1954;[42] Singh 1974[43]), Industries (Barthakur 1978;[44] Mali & Deka 1987;[45] Shri Prakash 1984[46]) and Marketing (Mohapatra 1989[47] & 1996[48]). The general pattern is eclectic, extensive in coverage, but except a few, have of little applied implications.

### *Population and Social Geography*

Population geography and lately, Social geography appear some of the major focal areas of predoctoral/ doctoral research in universities in the region. At doctoral level Bhuyan (1977) dealt with immigrants in Darrang district of Assam, Das (1975) studied the tribal population in Kamrup district, Goel (1983) studied the demographic structure of the region as a whole, Kumar (1982) dealt with the population of Nagaland, Mathew (1983) on spatio-temporal analysis of population of Meghalaya, Singh (1986) on population of Manipur, Singh (1989) on comparative population study of tribes and non-tribes of Manipur, Bora (1990) on Population of Siang region of Arunachal Pradesh and Pachau (1992) on population of Mizoram. Practically, all the states and a number of district level studies have been completed on a variety of issues like population growth and distribution, migration, composition (tribal/non-tribal, sex composition etc.) and other related processes.

Professional publications are also numerous. Some important studies on density and distribution are: (Taher, 1976;[49] Bora, 1990;[50] Borooah, 1985;[51] Kumar, 1983;[52] Mitra et al., 1971;[53] Sarma et al., 1989[54]) on growth dynamics of population (Bhuyan, 1973;[55] Butola, 1990;[56] Goel et al., 1981;[57] Sharma 1988[58]), on migration issues (Bhuyan, 1971;[59] Taher, 1987[60]), on demographic attributes (Das 1982[61]), on social geographic attributes (Bhattacharyya, 1990;[62] Bora et al., 1987;[63] Das et al., 1971–2;[64] Qureshi et al., 1984;[65] Sarma, 1989;[66] Taher (1977,[67] 1979,[68] 1994[69]), Lanusosang, 1989;[70] Das, 1986;[71] Goswami, 1989;[72] Qureshi, 1990;[73] Singh, 1979[74] and Singh 1980[75]).

### *Settlement Geography: Urban*

Urban geography has been, traditionally, a major focal area, globally speaking. In the Northeast region also there has been several pre-doctoral and doctoral studies on various aspects of urbanisation and morphological studies on cities. Mahanta (1986) studied the rural-urban fringe of Shillong, Nengnong (1991) analysed the rural-urban migration, Chakravaty (1992) looked at the rural-urban linkages of Shillong, Saikia (1991) studied the efficacy of the transport network of Shillong, Nongrum (1993) analysed the informal markets of Shillong, Singh (1995) on urban poverty alleviation programmes and public policy in Manipur and Das (1997) analysed the quality of life of the urban poor in Shillong. Singh (1971) studied the urban landscape around the small upper-Assam town of Dibrugarh; Bhattacharjya (1977) analysed the urban morphology of Guwahati; Singh (1981) studied the Imphal City and Jhunjhunwala (1989) studied the rural-urban linkages in Khasi and Jaintia Hills.

Professional publication in urban geography are fairly numerous. Bhattacharjya (1970,[76] 1976,[77] 1978,[78] 1979[79] and 1981[80]) studied various aspects of growth and morphology of Guwahati City. Sharma (1970,[81] 1979[82]) studied the pattern of urbanisation in Assam; Singh (1990)[83] on hierarchy of urban centres of Manipur; Sharma and Das (1976)[84] provided a functional classification of urban centres of Assam; Sharma (1982)[85] provided a structural analysis of Guwahati. Singh (1982)[86] studied the evolution and morphology of Shillong. Mohapatra (1990)[87] studied the comparative urban growth and urbanisation of the region at the district level, Chakravarty (1992)[88] provided an analytical construct for urban growth of Shillong, Nengnong et al. (1991[89] & 1994[90]) on rural-urban migration, Mohapatra et al. (1995a[91] & b[92]) on literacy in slums of Shillong and poverty in small towns (Tura).

*Settlement Geography: Rural*

The region being predominantly rural has attracted attention on the evolution, spatial organisation and development of rural areas of the region. Doctoral studies include Sharma (1983) on market centres in central Assam, Rahman (1997) on spatial organisation of rural settlements in Dhubri district, Yaden (1997) on unemployment in rural Nagaland and a number of pre-doctoral level studies.

Publications in books and professional journals include, Barthakur (1979)[93] on service centres in Brahmaputra Valley, Barthakur (1981)[94] on distributional pattern of rural settlements, Bhattacharjya (1979)[95] on central places of Darrang district, Qureshi (1981)[96] on rural ecology of Garo hills, Panda et al. (1982)[97] on rural settlements of Tirap district, Singh (1980[98]) on Metei settlements of Manipur valley, and Sharma et al. (1985[99]) on ranking and grouping of service centres of Nowgong.

### Historical and Political Geography

Historical geography and geographers are a vanishing tribe in the country — a country that boasts of a five thousand years old history, that reconstructing the geographies of periods and places have attracted no attention of geographers. On the other hand, political geography and geographers do thrive. Chander (1985) analysed the Naga insurgency. Choudhury (1987) attempted a politico-historical perspective for the North-East India. Varte (1989) analysed the Hmar political-geographic perspective, Singh (1991) the political geography of Mizoram.

Professional publications are more numerous. Bhattacharjya et al. (1973)[100] studied the historical geography of Kamarupa, Choudhury et al. (1983),[101] the geo-political significance of the McMahon Line, Gopalakrishnan (1985,[102] 86,[103] 88[104] and 90[105]) dealt with insurgency, the Assam students' uprising, problems of state formation etc. Sarma (1987)[106] dealt with the 'Pragjyotishapura', Singh (1972)[107] on the Puranic background of the North East and literatures are available on varied themes.

### Regional Development and Regional Planning

Lately geographers in the region have been addressing to the problem of underdevelopment and on appropriate public policy towards development of the region. Doctoral research in this direction was started by Mohapatra (1982), a study of evaluating the Myrdalian cummulative causation and divergence-convergence hypothesis. Saikia (1997) studied the export base theory and its applicability to the Northeast.

Books and professional publications are fairly extensive. Mohapatra (1977,[108] 1978[109] and 1980[110]) tested a new method of evaluating regional inequality. Munshi and Guha (1981[111]) specifically studied the causes of intra-regional inequality in the North East. Rai, Mohapatra et al. (1990)[112] put together the problems of hill areas of the region. Borthakur (1984)[113] formulated a strategy for the development of the Northeast, Pathak (1988[114] and 1990[115]) on development strategy, Singh et al. (1986)[116] on integrated area planning in Chandel district of Manipur, Taher (1977)[117] analysed the economic geographic basis of regional planning for the North East and Vandre Velde (1979)[118] on the ecological basis of development.

There is also a large number of research monographs on synthetic micro-regional studies and books on regional structure and geography of states and often on lower order regional units. It may not be possible to outline all that in this paper alone. However, they provide a continued basis of unraveling the regional synthesis and for instructional inculcation of students—if not duplicating gazetteer re-writing.

## Trends

On the basis of the survey and review of literature carried out the following trends in teaching and research in geography in the region could be discerned.

1. Starting with the early seventies, there has been a tremendous horizontal expansion in teaching (at undergraduate and post-graduate levels) and research publications and book production in geography —*prima facie*, the increasing popularity of the subject could be observed.
2. Whereas across disciplinary studies have increased in numbers, the potential of inter-disciplinary dialogue is limited. But this could apply to other social science disciplines as well.
3. Many of the researches are repetitious, i.e., the large number of regional monographs without further insights or additional points of interest. Quality of such writings could improve with genuine inter-disciplinary inputs.
4. Geographers in the region use methodologies of both empiricist social scientists of both on "nomothetic nature" as well as "ideographic character", latter, as in the case of regional monograph writing, but relatively less on developing newer methodologies and methods of empirical research, the subject being a field based one. This needs added attention.
5. Though publications have proliferated, majority are confined to regional literature — they need to be exposed to national and international (literature in the subject). This, of course, requires further qualitative improvements in methodology and focused, with improved presentation quality (in maps, diagrams etc).

6. Theory remains, by and large, a problem area. With the variations and variety that the North East provides, new ideas, interpretations and explanations are expected, but not reflected in actual research output from the geography community in the region.

At the global level, past three decades in geography have been path-breaking and highly productive, particularly in seminal contributions in *theory and epistemological researches*, geography as (social) *problem-solving discipline*, seminal studies *in man-environment relationships,* in which many physical geographers have started integrating their works with contemporary environmental issues and also, in areas of developing and using high technology in applied researches in geography. Though the recent Indian contributions in geography is falling within the latter three areas, theory generation and epistemological discourses in Indian geography has been practically absent. The same could be true of the trend in geographic research and teaching in the Northeast Region, also. This is largely, perhaps because of the fact that the geographic discourse in India and particularly in the Northeast is yet to discover its contextual moorings. If new insights and theory generation is to be promoted, geographers have to discover the *context for discourse.* For the Northeast, the *ethnic plurality* and the *environmental diversity* provides precisely, such contexts for relevant research and theory generation. Ultimately, after all, the original agenda of geographic discourse is directly relevant in the context of the Northeast, — *the biological perspective and the anthropogenic view.*[119]

**ENDNOTES**

1. D.R. Stoddart (1986), *On Geography*, Basil-Blackwell, London.
2. A. Ahmad (1996), *Progress in Indian Geography*, Status Report presented to the 28th International Geographical Congress, The Hague, Indian National Science Academy, New Delhi, pp. 9–10.
3. Largely the Ph.D. monographs have been carried out at the Gauhati University (about 30) and North-Eastern Hill University (about 20), the other University departments being new and the initial stages of their research programmes.

4. In NEHU alone, more than 20 such research projects have been completed in the Department of Geography, over the last 22 years of its existence.
5. T.S. Kuhn (1970), *The Structure of Scientific Revolution*, Chicago Univ. Press, 2nd. Ed., Chicago.
6. D. Harvey (1969), *Explanations in Geography*, Edward Arnold Pub. Ltd., G.B.
7. Galois, Bob (1976), "Ideology and the Idea of Nature: The case of Prince Kropotkin", *Anipode(8)*, pp. 1–16, repinted in Richard Peet (ed.), *Radical Geography*, Methuen, UK, pp. 66–94.
8. For example the influence of Darwin and his evolutionary paradigm on the first generation geographers. See, D.R. Stoddart (1982), "Darwin's Impact on Geography", AAG.
9. Clarence Glacken (1967), *Traces on the Rhodian Shores: Nature and Culture in Western Thought from Ancient Times to the End of Eighteenth Century*, Berkeley, Cali.
10. S.P. Chatterjee (1936), *Le Plateau de Meghalaya*, Les Presses Modernes, Paris and H.P. Das (1954), unplublished Ph.D. dissertation to LSEPS, London. Interestingly, the name Meghalaya for the new state carved out of Assam with the Khasi and Jaintia Hill District and the Garo Hill District was picked up from no where else than the thesis of Prof. Chatterjee.
11. Starting with William Bunge at Chicago, who was thrown out of the University because of his radical views, and opted to drive a taxi!
12. Mohapatra, A.C. (1988) *Dynamics in land use and soil characteristics under sub-tropical rain forest and grasslands : a dignostic study of the West Khasi Hills District of Meghalaya*, Technical Report, sponsored by DOEF, Govt. of India, (Unpublished).
13. Mohapatra, A.C. (1997), *Soil Erosion in Umran Basin of Meghalaya*, Technical Report, sponsored by S&T Cell, Dept. of Planning, Govt. of Meghalaya, Shillong (1991–1993, completed in 1997: unpublished).
14. Rai, R.K. (1997), Technical Report on *Environmental Degradation in Coal Mining Areas of Meghalaya*, sponsored by Ministry of Env. and Forests, GOI. (Unpublished)
15. Mohapatra, A.C. and Konwar, M. (1993), "Landscape Approach to Land Classification: Study of a river basin in Meghalaya", Geographical Review of India, (55:1), pp. 80–91.
16. Mohapatra, A.C. and Konwar, M. (1989), "Analysis of Soil Rating Indices in the West Khasi Hills District of Meghalaya", paper submitted for publication in *Indian Journal of Regional Science*, (21:2), IIT, Kharagpur, pp. 10–20. (Jointly with M. Konwar)
17. Mohapatra, A.C. and Konwar, M. (1995),"Deforestation and Soil Erosion in Umran Basin: Peoples' Response to Ecological Issues", Proc. *National Seminar on Environmental Degradation in Eastern & North-Eastern Himalaya*, Centre for Himalayan Studies, North Bengal University, Siliguri, October 7–8, 1996 (Proc., forthcoming).
18. Mohapatra, A.C. and Konwar, M. (1996), "Slope-Mass Movement and Associated Soils in East Khasi and Jaintia Hills of Meghalaya", *Journal of the Indian Society of Soil Sciences*, IARI, Vol. 44, No. 4, Dec–1996, pp. 712–717. (Jointly with U. Baruah)).

19. Mohapatra, A.C. and Konwar, M. (1997), "Pricing Urban Water Supply: The Political Economy of Distributive Justice vs. Efficiency of Service", *Proc. Seminar on Water and Water Resource Management in North-East India*, May 6–7, 1997, Shillong, India (in Proc., forthcoming)
20. Mohapatra, A.C. and Konwar, M. (1997), "Traditional Rights, Community Participation for Sustainable Forest Management in North-Eastern Region, India", *Himalayan Paryavaran*, Darjeeling, India, Vol.5, pp. 35–36.
21. Rai, R.K. and Agarwal, M. (1993), "Geo-Environmental Hazards around Umiam Lake", *Applied Geomorphology in Tropics*, P.R. Sharma (ed.), Rishi Publ., Varanasi, pp. 73–78.
22. See, annexture for details of studies cited.
23. Barman, R. and Das, M.M. (1978), "Crop Combination Regions of Assam", NEG(10), pp. 15–22.
24. Mohapatra, A.C. (1978), "Some aspects of green revolution and concentration of crop out-put; region-wise, cropwise, pricewise and classwise in India", *North Eastern Economic Review*, (3:3), pp. 194–202.
25. Bhagabati, A.K. (Levels of Agricultural Productivity in the Brahmaputra Valley", *NEG(16)*, pp. 30–38.
26. Chattoraj, S. and Sahu, R. (1983), "Inter-district variations in agricultural productivity, etc.", *HG(2:1)*, pp. 21–25.
27. Das, M.M. (1984), *Peasant Agriculture in Assam*, Inter-India, New Delhi.
28. Gopalakrishnan, R. (1989), "The State of Agricultural Development in Assam", GRI(51:2), pp. 62–67.
29. Goswami, D.C. (1989), "Floods and Their Impact on Agriculture of Assam", in P.C. Goswami (ed.), *Agriculture in Assam*, Inst. of Dev. Studies, Guwahati. pp. 191–207.
30. Rai, R.K. and Panda, P.C. (1983), "Hill Slope Farming around Shillong", *Environmental Management*, Allahbad University, Allahabad.
31. Shukla, S.P. (1983), *Agricultural Potential and Planning in Hill Region in India*, Chugh Publ., New Delhi.
32. Singh, R.P. (1977), "Development of Irrigation Potential and its Utilisation in Manipur", *NEG(9)*, pp. 32–37.
33. Singh, R.R. (1985), "Land Capability Classification of the Manipur Valley", GRI(47:4), pp. 59–66.
34. Bhagabati, A.K. (1986), "A Spatial Appraisal of Land and Natural Vegetation in North-East India", *NEG*(18:1&2), pp. 67–77.
35. Mohapatra, A.C. and Alempokba, I. (1982), "Landuse in a Naga Village, Ungma", *Himalaya* (6:7), pp. 13–19.
36. Mohapatra, A.C., and Haloi, K. (1985), "Landuse Classification in Tribal and Hill Areas of Khasi Hills", in A.B. Mukerjee and A. Ahmad. (ed.), *India: Culture, Society and Economy*, Inter-India, New Delhi, pp. 651–661.
37. Mohapatra, A.C., et al. (1992), "Environmental Planning for a Hill District etc.", in *Behavioural Dimensions of Tribal Landscape, Vol. 4.*, G.P. Gupta (ed.), Arihant, Jaipur, pp. 138–150.
38. Baruah, U. et al. (1988), "An Appraisal of Soil and Land Resources of North Eastern Region", HG(7:1&2), pp. 21–26.
39. Goswami, D.C. (1992), Water Resources of North-East India, *Planning Perspectives for the North-Eastern and Eastern Zone*, Malcolm S. Adiseshiah (ed.), Lancer Pub. Pvt. Ltd., New Delhi,

40. Mohapatra, A.C. (1992), "Zonal Planning in Power Development", *Planning Perspectives for the North-Eastern and Eastern Zone*, Malcolm S. Adiseshiah (ed.), Lancer Pub. Pvt. Ltd. , New Delhi, pp. 25–46.
41. Chandra, S. (1984), "Mineral Resource Utilisation in North-East India", *HG(3:1)*, pp. 17–19.
42. Das, H.P. (1954), op. cit.
43. Singh, R.P. (1974), "Forest Resources of Manipur", *NEG(6:1&2)*.
44. Barthakur, M. (1978), "Industrial Inertia etc.", NEG(10:1&2), pp. 1–6.
45. Mali, D.D. and Deka, P. (1987) (ed.), *Industrial Development in North-East India*, Omsons, Guwahati.
46. Shri Prakash (1984), "Capital Coefficient in Small Industries in Meghalaya", *HG(3:1)*, pp. 1–15.
47. Mohapatra, A.C. (1989), "Location Pattern of Markets in Pre- and Early British Period in North East India", *Sem. Proc.* of NEIHA, pp. 341–347.
48. Mohapatra, A.C. (1996), "Marketing, Global Integration and Development: Scenario for Developing Countries with Specific Reference to India", *Proc. of International Seminar on Marketing & Development, Saitama University, Japan*, (ed.) Dr. Kazuo Usui, Faculty of Economics, Saitama University, pp. 113–124.
49. Taher, M. (1976), "The Geo-Economic Basis of Population Distribution in Mangadoi Sub-division", NEG(8), pp. 8–13.
50. Bora, H.N. (1990), "Distribution and Density of Pattern of Population in Siang Region", *NEG(22:1&2)* pp. 41–49.
51. Borooah, G.L. (1985), *Population Geography of Assam, A case study of Dibrugarh district, Mittal*, New Delhi.
52. Kumar, G. (1983), "Nagaland: A study in Environmental Determinism of Population Distribution", *Indian Geographical Studies, Research Bulletin (20)*, pp. 38-42.
53. Mitra, S. and Singh, D.K. (1971), "Indexes of Population Concentration and Temporal Redistribution in the brahmaputra Valley", *GRI(33:1)*, pp. 15–21.
54. Sarma, S.N. and Bhagabati, A.K. (1989), "Impact of Slope on Population Distribution and Land-use in Boko Thana Area of Assam", *NEG(21:1&2)*, pp. 25–34.
55. Bhuyan, M.C. (1973), "Trends of Population Growth in Assam", *NEG(5:1&2)*, pp. 24–34.
56. Butola, B.S. (1990), "Population Dynamics and Socio-Economic Development in North-Eastern India", in M.C.Pandey (ed.), *Population Awareness, Series-V*, NEHU, Shillong, pp. 31–41.
57. Goel, N.P. et al. (1981), "Trends of Population Growth in Meghalaya", *Social Sciences*, Jr. of NERC-ICSSR, Shillong.
58. Sharma, H.N. (1988), "Pattern of Present Population Growth and its impact on Assam", NEG(20:1&2), pp. 12–16.
59. Bhuyan, M.C. (1971), "Immigration to Assam Valley: A geographical Analysis", NEG(3:1), pp. 177–89.
60. Taher, M. (1987), "Population Base of Assam", *NEG(19)*, pp. 1–16.
61. Das, M.M. (1982), "Demographic Structure of Assam", *Gauhati Univ. Jr. of Sciences, (28)*, pp. 52–60.
62. Bhattacharjya, N.N. (1990), "Linguistic and Tribal Regions of North East India", in R.B. Mandal (ed.), *Pattern of Regional Geography*, Concept, New Delhi, pp. 145–58.

63. Bora, H.N. and Sharma, H.N. (1987), "Distribution Pattern of Population and Social Groups in Arunachal Pradesh", NEG(19), pp. 17–28.
64. Das, D. and Singh, D.K. (1971-2), "Tribal Population in Guwahati", NEG(3&4), pp. 19–27.
65. Qureshi, Z.H. and Ganguly, P. (1984), "Relative proportions of tribals and non-tribals in North-East India", in Karotempral, S. (ed.), *Tribes in North East India*, Vendrame Missiological Institute, pp. 30–39.
66. Sarma, S.S. (1989), "Spatio-temporal distribution of tribes of NE India with special reference to Assam", *Proc. of NEIHA*, Shillong.
67. Taher, M. (1977), "Tribes of North-East India: A Diagnostic Survey in spatial pattern", *NEG(9),* pp. 16–24.
68. Taher, M. (1979), "Scheduled Caste Population of Assam: A Spatial Analysis", *NEG(11),* pp. 19–27.
69. Taher, M. (1994), "Tribes of North-East India", *Prajna(4),* GU, Guwahati, pp. 1–8.
70. Lanusosang, T. (1989), *Nagaland, A Study in Social Geography,* Directorate of School Education, Nagaland, Kohima.
71. Das, N.R. (1986), "Determinants and Correlates of spatial pattern of tribal literacy in North East India", HG(5), pp. 1–12.
72. Goswami, G.C. (1989), "Literacy among the tribals of Darrang district, Assam", NEG(21), pp. 49–56.
73. Qureshi, Z.H. (1990), "Human Geography of the Monpa. A Resume", Bhuvid (1:1), pp. 30–33.
74. Singh, D.K. (1979), "Taki-Lalung: An Adi Tribal Village in Siang district of Arunachal Pradesh", in *Habitat Asia, (1)*, Concept, New Delhi, pp. 148–51.
75. Singh, R.P. (1980), "Tangkhul Nagas of Manipur: Their Habitat, Economy and Society", GRI (42), pp. 216–28.
76. Bhattacharjya, N.N. (1970), "Urban Morphology of Gauhati", *Jr. of NE India Geographical Society (2:2)*, pp. 141–150.
77. Bhattacharjya, N.N. (1976), "Mangaldoi: A Study in Urban Morphology", *NEG(8)*, pp. 15–20.
78. Bhattacharjya, N.N. (1978), "Population Density Gradient of Guwahati City", *NEG(10),* pp. 7–14.
79. Bhattacharjya, N.N. (1979), "Growth and Spatial Structure of Guwahati City", *Indian Geographical Studies, Research Bulletin(13)*, pp. 40–44.
80. Bhattacharjya, N.N. (1981), *Morphology of the Towns of Assam with special reference to the City of Gauhati: An Analytico-Synthetic Study,* Mani-Manik Prakashan, Guwahati.
81. Sharma, H.N. (1970), "Pattern of Urbanisation in Assam", *Jr. of NE India Geographical Society (2:1)*, pp. 83–94.
82. Sharma, H.N. (1979), "Urban Growth and Spatial Pattern etc.", NEG(2), pp. 28–47.
83. Singh, N.D. (1990), "Hierarchy of Urban Centres of Manipur", NEG(22), pp. 33–40.
84. Sharma, M.C. and Das, H.P. (1976), "The Functional Pattern and Classification of Urban Centres etc.", NEG(8), pp. 1–7.
85. Sharma, M.C. (1982), *Structural Analysis of the City of Guwahati: A Geographical Study,* Naya Prakashan, Calcutta.

86. Singh, J.P. (1982), *Growth and Morphology of Shillong*, Concept, New Delhi.
87. Mohapatra, A.C. (1990), *Growth of Urban Population in North East Region (1951–1981),* U.G.C. Population Education Programme and Centre for Adult and Continuing Education, NEHU, Shillong. (Mimeo).
88. Chakravarty, N. and Mohapatra, A.C. (1992), "Peripheral Urban Development: An analytical model with specific reference to Shillong" in *Urbanisation and Development in North-East India*, J.B. Ganguly (ed.), New Delhi, pp. 22–28.
89. Nengnong, D.D., Nayak, D.K. and Mohapatra, A.C. (1992), Process of Urbanisation in Meghalaya: Evidences in Rural to Urban Migration", in *Urbanisation and Development in North-East India*, J.B.Ganguly (ed.), New Delhi, pp. 237–252.
90. Nengnong, D.D., Nayak, D.K. and Mohapatra, A.C. (1994), "Patterns of Migration in Meghalaya with special reference to Rural-Urban stream", *Journal of NE India Geographical Society (24)*, pp. 71–82.
91. Mohapatra, A.C. and Marbaniang, N.V. (1995a), "Literacy and the Poor: A Study of Selected Slums of Shillong", *Proc. of Seminar on Population and Development,* NEICSSR, Shillong, India (forth-coming).
92. Mohapatra, A.C., Marbaniang, N.V. and Das, S. (1995b), "Urban Poverty and small towns: A case study of Tura Town of Meghalaya", (*Proc. of Seminar on Small Towns of North-East India, November 21, 1995 (ed.)*) (forth-coming).
93. Barthakur, M. (1979), "Growth and Development of Service Centres etc.", *NEG(2),* pp. 84–88.
94. Barthakur, S. (1981), "Distributional Pattern of Rural settlements on the Eastern Part of Tezpur sub-division", *NEG(13)*, pp. 13–19.
95. Bhattacharyya, N.N. (1979), "Central Places of Darrang District, Assam", *NEG(11),* pp. 70–73.
96. Qureshi, Z.H. (1981), "Ecology of Rural Settlements in Garo Hills", *Social Research(1:2)*, pp. 12–22.
97. Panda, P.C. and Yadav, K. (1982), "A Study of Rural Settlements of Tirap District, Arunachal Pradesh", HG(2:2), pp. 20–31.
98. Singh, K.Y. (1980), "The Evolution of Metei Settlements in the Valley of Manipur", NEG(12), pp. 39–44.
99. Sharma, P and Sharma, H.N. (1985), "Identification, Ranking and Grouping of Service Centres — A Case Study of Nowgong District", NEG(17), pp. 12–20.
100. Bhattacharyya, N.N. and Taher, M. (1973), "Kamrupa: A Study in Historical Geography", *Jr. of NE India Geographical Society (5)*, pp. 8–15.
101. Choudhury, J.D. and Bhattacharyya, N.N. (1983), "Geopolitical Significance of the McMahon Line", *NEG(15),* pp. 55–58.
102. Gopalakrishnan, R. (1985), "A Geographic View of Insurgency in the North-East India", *NEHU Jr. of SS, (3:3).*
103. Gopalakrishnan, R. (1986), "Geographical Aspects of Crisis in the Brahmaputra Valley (Assam)", *The Indian Journal of Pol. Sc. (48:3).*
104. Gopalakrishnan, R. (1988), "Background to the Notions of Territories in North-Eastern Region of India", *NEHU Jr. of SS, (6:2).*

105. Gopalakrishnan, R. (1990), "Process of State Formation in the North-Eastern Region of India", in R.K. Rai, Mohapatra, A.C. et al. (ed), *Hill Area Development*, GSNER, Shillong.
106. Sarma, S.S. (1987), "Pragjyotishpura — the Ancient Capital of Assam", *Proc. of NEIHA*, Shillong.
107. Singh, I.D. (1972), "The Brahmaputra: A Study in Puranic Geography", *Jr. of NE India Geographical Society (3–5)*, pp. 32–39.
108. Mohapatra, A.C., Goel, N.P. et al. (1977), " A study of spatial-sectoral imbalances in Meghalaya", *North-Eastern Geographer*, (9), pp. 9–15.
109. Mohapatra, A.C., Goel, N.P. et al. (1978) "An alternative model of measuring divergent-convergent hypothesis: A study of Regional Per Capita Incomes In India", *Indian Journals of Regional Sciences*, (10:2), pp. 39–50.
110. Mohapatra, A.C., Goel, N.P. et al. and Shri Prakash (1980), "Economic development in the State of Madhya Pradesh, India", *Third World Planning Review*, (2:1), Liverpool, U.K., pp. 91–106.
111. Munshi, S.K. and Guha, A. (1984), "Levels of Regional Development in the North-East", Annal (of NAGI), (4).
112. Rai, R.K., Mohapatra, A.C. et al. (1990: ed.), *Hill Area Development*, GSNEHR, Shillong.
113. Barthakur, M. (1984), "Formulation of Planning and Development Strategies for North East India", *NEG* (16), pp. 47–54.
114. Pathak, C.R. (1988), "Development Strategy for North-Eastern Region", in P. Thakur (ed.), *Profile of a Development Strategy for India's North-East*, Span Publ., Guwahati, pp. 111–119.
115. Pathak, C.R. (1990), "Development Strategy for North-Eastern Region", in Rai, R.K., Mohapatra, A.C. et al. (ed.), *Hill Area Development*, GSNEHR, Shillong, pp. 36–45.
116. Singh, R.P. and Devi, H.G. (1986), Approach to Integrated Area Planning and Stategy for development etc", *Transactions of ICG* (16), pp. 47–55.
117. Taher, M. (1977), "Geo-Economic Basis of Regional Planning in North East India", *North Eastern Economic Review (1:3)*.
118. Vandre Velde, E.J. (1979), "The Role of Ecology in the Development Geography of North-Eastern India", NEG(11), pp. 1–18.
119. Here the "anthropogenic view" is purposefully differentiated from the "anthropocentric view", the latter emphasising on a "man-centred paradigm" and the former, uses the Darwinian framework of "man among the rest of the living nature", — a view that "naturalises man and humanises nature".

(N.B. Abbreviation of names of professional journals used: GRI: Geographical Review of India, NEG: The North Eastern Geographer, HG: Hill Geographer)

ANNEXURE I

# List of Research Monographs Cited

## A. Environment and Society

1. Konwar, M. (1990), *Land Classification in Hill Areas: A Study of West Khasi Hills District, Meghalaya*, Ph.D. dissertation submitted to North-Eastern Hill University, Shillong (unpublished).
2. Qureshi, Z.H. (1990), *Geo-ecology of Kameng Himalaya: A Study into Ecosystem and Human Response*, Ph.D. dissertation submitted to M.L. Sukhadia University, Udaipur (unpublished).
3. Baruah, Utpal (1994), *Slope Mass Movement and Associated Soils in East-Khasi and Jaintia Hills of Meghalaya*, Ph.D. dissertation submitted to North-Eastern Hill University, Shillong (unpublished).

## B. Geomorphology

1. Pattanaik, S.N. (1979), *Geomorphology and Agricultural Development in Meghalaya*, M.Phil. dissertation submitted to North-Eastern Hill University, Shillong (unpublished).
2. Panda, Girish (1986), *Geomorphology and Agricultural Land Use Capability Classification in Mawsynram Region*, Ph.D. dissertation submitted to North-Eastern Hill University, Shillong (unpublished).
3. Agarwal, Mandira (1995), *Geomorphology and Environmental Management of Umiam Basin, East-Khasi Hills, Meghalaya*, Ph.D. dissertation submitted to North-Eastern Hill University, Shillong (unpublished).
4. Rinawma, P. (1987), *Geomorphology and Agricultural Development in Lunglei district, Mizoram*, Ph.D. dissertation submitted to North-Eastern Hill University, Shillong (unpublished).

## C. Agricultural Geography

1. Aziz, Abdul (1981), *Measurement of Agricultural Productivity —A case study of Mewat*, Ph.D. dissertation submitted to North-Eastern Hill University, Shillong (unpublished).
2. Das, M.M. (1982), *Peasant Agriculture in Assam*, Ph.D. dissertation submitted to Gauhati University, Guwahati (Published with the same title, Inter-India, Delhi, 1984).
3. Datta, L. (1983), *Agricultural Occupance of Nagaon District: A Spatio-Temporal Analysis*, Ph.D. dissertation submitted to Gauhati University, Guwahati (unpublished).
4. Sahu, R. (1984), *Diffusion and Distributional Patterns of HYV in Lower Brahmaputra Valley*, Ph.D. dissertation submitted to North-Eastern Hill University, Shillong (unpublished).
5. Chattaraj, S. (1985), *Emerging Patterns of Agricultural Landuse in Kamrup District*, Ph.D. dissertation submitted to North-Eastern Hill University, Shillong (unpublished).
6. Mipun, B.S. (1987), *Immigrants and Agricultural Development in Lower Brahmaputra Valley,* Ph.D. dissertation submitted to North-Eastern Hill University, Shillong (unpublished).
7. Shukla, S.P. (1983), *Agricultural Potential and Planning in a Hill Region in India*, Chugh Publ., Allahabad. (This is a version of his Ph.D. thesis, the details of which could not be ascertained)
8. Saikia, H. (1994), *Patterns of Land Holding and Agricultural Productivity of Upper Brahmaputra Valley of Assam*, Ph.D. dissertation submitted to North-Eastern Hill University, Shillong (unpublished).
9. Bhagabati, AK. (1990), *Spatial Analysis of Small-scale Agriculture in Assam: A Case Study of Nalbari District*, Ph.D. dissertation submitted to Gauhati University, Guwahati (unpublished).

## D. Geography of Resources, Manufacturing and Marketing

1. Borah, B.B. (1984), *Impact of Technological Innovation in the Tea Industry: A Case Study of Jorhat Sub-division*, M.Phil

dissertation submitted to Gauhati University, Guwahati. (unpublished).

2. Tahbildar, M. (1986), *Emerging Industrial Set-up and its Impact on the Socio-Economic Structure of Jagiroad Area,* M.Phil dissertation submitted to Gauhati University, Guwahati (unpublished).
3. Borah, J. (1988), *Pattern of Cooking Energy Use in Guwahati Municipal Area,* M.Phil dissertation submitted to Gauhati University, Guwahati (unpublished).
4. Kharkonger, S. (1989), *Industrial Geography of Meghalaya,* M.Phil. dissertation submitted to North-Eastern Hill University, Shillong (unpublished).
5. Borthakur, M. (1994), *Periodic Market System: A Comparative Study in Tribal and Non-Tribal Areas in the Northeast,* Ph.D. dissertation submitted to North-Eastern Hill University, Shillong (unpublished).
6. Pio, S. (1990), *Socio-Physical Factors in the Development of Tea Industry in Assam: A Case Study of Three Tea Estates,* M.Phil. dissertation submitted to North-Eastern Hill University, Shillong (unpublished).
7. Colney, R. (1996), *Industrial Development in Mizoram,* Ph.D. dissertation submitted to North-Eastern Hill University, Shillong (published).

## E. Population and Social Geography

1. Bhuyan, M.C. (1977), *Immigrant Population in Assam: An Analytico Synthetic Study with Special Treatment of Darrang District,* Ph.D. dissertation submitted to Gauhati University, Guwahati (unpublished).
2. Das, D. (1975), *Tribal Population and Settlement in Kamrup with Special Reference to the Concentration in the Southern Region,* Ph.D. dissertation submitted to Utkal University, Bhubaneswar (unpublished).
3. Goel, N.P. (1983), *Demographic Structure of North-East India,* Ph.D. dissertation submitted to North-Eastern Hill University, Shillong (unpublished).
4. Kumar, G. (1982), *Population Structure of Nagaland,* Ph.D. dissertation submitted to Patna University, Patna (unpublished).

5. Mathew, T.K. (1983), *Spatio-Temporal Analysis of Population of Meghalaya*, Ph.D. dissertation submitted to Gauhati University, Guwahati (unpublished).
6. Singh, A.K.S. (1986), *Population of Manipur: Geographical Analysis*, Ph.D. dissertation submitted to Gauhati University, Guwahati (unpublished).
7. Singh, H.B. (1989), *A Comprehensive Study of Socio-Economic Transformation of Tribal and Non-tribal People of Manipur during Post-independence Period*, Ph.D. dissertation submitted to Gauhati University, Guwahati (unpublished).
8. Bora, H.N. (1990), *Population of Siang Region: A Geographical Analysis*, Ph.D. dissertation submitted to Gauhati University, Guwahati (unpublished).
9. Pachau, L. (1992), *Population of Mizoram: A Geographical Analysis*, Ph.D. dissertation submitted to North-Eastern Hill University, Shillong.

## F. Settlement Geography: Urban

1. Mahanta, H.B. (1986), *Continuity and Change: A Geographical Analysis of the Urban of Shillong UA*, M.Phil. dissertation submitted to North-Eastern Hill University, Shillong (unpublished).
2. Nengnong, D.D. (1991), *Rural Urban Migration in Meghalaya*, M.Phil. dissertation submitted to North-Eastern Hill University, Shillong (unpublished).
3. Saikia, Anup (1991), *Road Network and Traffic Density in Shillong*, M.Phil. dissertation submitted to North-Eastern Hill University, Shillong (unpublished).
4. Chakravarty, Nandini (1992), *Rural Urban Linkages and Interactions: A case study of Shillong and its hinterland*, M.Phil. dissertation submitted to North-Eastern Hill University, Shillong (unpublished).
5. Nongrum, Kwilly (1993), *Urban Informal Sector in Shillong*, M.Phil. dissertation submitted to North-Eastern Hill University, Shillong (unpublished).
6. Singh, L. Sunil (1995), *Urban Poverty Alleviation and Public Policy: An Evaluative Study of Imphal Valley (Manipur)*,

M.Phil. dissertation submitted to North-Eastern Hill University, Shillong (unpublished).

7. Das, Susmita (1997), *Quality of Life and the Urban Poor: A case study of the city of Shillong*, M.Phil. dissertation submitted to North-Eastern Hill University, Shillong (unpublished).
8. Singh, D.K. (1971), *Dibrugarh and its Environs: A study in quantitative analysis of the urban landscape of the region*, Ph.D. dissertation submitted to Gauhati University, Guwahati (unpublished).
9. Bhattacharyya, N.N. (1977), *Gauhati: A study in urban morphology*, Ph.D. dissertation submitted to Utkal University, Bhubaneswar (unpublished).
10. Singh, M.B. (1981), *Imphal: A study in urban geography*, Ph.D. dissertation submitted to Gauhati University, Guwahati (unpublished).
11. Jhunjhunwala, K.K. (1989), *Rural-urban Interaction and Pattern of Linkages in the Khasi and Jaintia Hills Area*, Ph.D. dissertation submitted to Gauhati University, Guwahati (unpublished).
12. Sarma, S.S. (1989), *The growth problems of the Guwahati City and its regional impact*, Ph.D. dissertation submitted to North-Eastern Hill University, Shillong (unpublished).

**G. Settlement Geography: Rural**

1. Sharma, P.K. (1983), *Market Centres in Central Assam: A Geographical Analysis*, Ph.D. dissertation submitted to Gauhati University, Guwahati (unpublished).
2. Rahman, M. (1996), *Settlement Structure of Dhuburi district*, Ph.D. dissertation submitted to Gauhati University, Guwahati (unpublished).
3. Yaden, S. (1997), *Work and Employment in Taditional Society*, Ph.D. dissertation submitted to North-Eastern Hill University, Shillong (unpublished).

**H. Historical and Political Geography**

1. Chander, S. (1985), *Nature and Pattern of Insurgency in Nagaland: A Geographical Analysis*, Ph.D. dissertation

submitted to North-Eastern Hill University, Shillong (unpublished).

2. Choudhury, J.D. (1987), *Politico-Historical Perspective of North East India etc.*, Ph.D. dissertation submitted to Gauhati University, Guwahati (unpublished).
3. Varte, L.K. (1989), *Historical and Political Geography of Hmars etc.*, M.Phil dissertation submitted to North-Eastern Hill University, Shillong (unpublished).
4. Singh, S.N. (1991), *Political Geography of Mizoram*, Ph.D. dissertation submitted to North-Eastern Hill University, Shillong (unpublished).

## I. Regional Development and Planning

1. Mohapatra, A.C. (1982), *Regional Inequality in India*, Ph.D. dissertation submitted to North-Eastern Hill University, Shillong (unpublished).
2. Saikia, A. (1997), *Regional Development of North-Eastern Region of India: Export Base Theory, Govt. Policy and Underdevelopment*, Ph.D. dissertation submitted to North-Eastern Hill University, Shillong (unpublished).

# 3

# North East India: Trends in Historical Writing 1947–1997

*D.R. Syiemlieh*

Historical studies on North East India may be traced to the early decades of the 19th Century,[1] though the historical sense was preserved by literate societies in their respective chronicles and non-literate communities in their folklore and oral tradition. Research into the region's history started with Edward Gait's historiographical study[2] and his popular *A History of Assam* written early this century which was sufficiently comprehensive given the time and material available to him. Historical research was dominated in the 1930s–1940s by S.K. Bhuyan whose works can be categorised into historical, biographical and miscellaneous. Between 1930–1938, he compiled, collated and edited 11 Buranjis; during these years and on to 1959, he authored 4 histories[3] apart from a whole variety of writing that was curiously both nationalistic and an acceptance of British rule. Bhuyan was a historian with a mission. Throughout his career he was a crusader for finding Assam a befitting place in the historical writing of India. He aired this view when in Cuttack, Orissa in 1953 and a year earlier as President of the Indian History Congress expressed that it was his "religious zeal to let the world know the great and good things of Assam which forms an integral part of Mother India".[4] Joined by Padmanath Bhattacharyya Vidyavinod, Benudhar Sharma, Hem Chandra Goswami, Kanak Lal Barua and Banikanta Kakati the historical writings on Assam moved from its nascent stage to details of a variety of histories. To a great extent this was made possible through the foundation of the Kamarupa Anusandhan Samiti (April 1912) and its journal (1933).

The post 1947 period did not immediately provide an opening for historical studies despite the changed political situation. It was some years before Assam's role in the freedom struggle was given attention. K.N. Dutt first drew notice with *Landmarks of the Freedom Struggle in Assam*, Guwahati, 1958 and Hem Barua centred on a particular phase with *The Nineteen Forty Two Upheaval in Assam*, Jorhat, 1964. Thereafter, there has been a veritable deluge of material on the freedom struggle in Assam with important contributions from Amalendu Guha, *Planter Raj to Swaraj Freedom Struggle and Electoral Politics in Assam 1826–47*, New Delhi, 1977; H.K. Barpujari et al. (ed.), *Political History of Assam*, Government of Assam, Gauhati, Vol. I, 1977, Vol. II, 1978, Vol. III, 1980; reference in Sumit Sarkar's widely acclaimed and readable *Modern India 1885–1947*, New Delhi, 1983, and R.C. Majumdar's edited *Struggle for Freedom*, Bombay, 1969. Research into this aspect of history continues to draw the inquiry of many younger historians in M.Phil., Ph.D. dissertations and in articles, particularly in the various *Proceedings of the North East India History Association*, too many to enumerate in this paper.[5] Amalendu Guha's Presidential Address to the Modern History Section of the Indian History Congress in 1984, is especially remembered for interweaving some aspects of the history of this region in his discussion of Indian nationalism in general.

There was little sense of Indian nationalism in the hills of North East India for historical reasons. Tirot Singh, Kiang Nangbah, Ropuiliani, Togan Sangma and Sonaram Sangma led resistances against the British has been fairly well covered in the general histories of the region. Recently however, due to the importance taken by histories of communities and the new states in the region a fresh interpretation is being sought to explain the role of these and other leaders as local national heroes — to use a term of Irfan Habib.[6] An historian has used a novel for historical data to draw attention to Tirot Singh's last days;[7] another eulogises this Khasi Chief as the "Greatest Freedom Fighter of North-Eastern Region" without making a comparative study of the struggle by other leaders.[8] One is reminded of the words of caution given by S.K. Barpujari that:[9]

> There has been a tendency in our local studies to magnify regional achievements, to exalt local heroes and to glorify local languages, customs and usages out of all proportion to their intrinsic value.

Reinterpretation of the events leading to India's independence and the incorporation of Manipur and the Khasi states into the Indian Union is under way. Scholars in Manipur have questioned the entire process of integration of the former princely state and if the sentiments of a section of Khasi society is considered pertinent, the integration of the 25 *Himas* into India in an Assam administration will be scrutinised.[10]

In part this trend in history is reflective of the over-emphasis on the history of Assam, and particularly that of the Brahmaputra valley to the neglect of the Barak valley, the hills between the valleys and the hill fringe. From Gait's history of Assam to S.L. Baruah, *A Comprehensive History of Assam*, New Delhi, 1985, the hill region is only referred to in passing and in Ahom relations with the tribal states and societies. It would require historians from among the Nagas, Khasis, Garos, from Cachar, Manipur and Tripura to fill in the lacunae in detail. But first the history of these areas may be traced to Abdul Ali's *Notes on Early History of Manipur* (1923), Verrier Elwin's *India's North-East Frontier in the Nineteenth Century*, Bombay, 1959, and *Nagas in the Nineteenth Century*, Bombay, 1969. The Jaintias had their first historian in S.M. Ali whose *History of Jaintia*, Dacca, 1954, made an attempt to narrate the history from both oral and written sources. As states and union territories were formed in the region in administrative reorganisations beginning 1950 with the Chief Commissionerships of Manipur and Tripura and subsequent changes with Nagaland's statehood (1963) and ushering in of the states of Tripura, Manipur, Meghalaya and the Union Territories of Mizoram and Arunachal Pradesh (1972), their history was given focus. M. Alemchiba's *A Brief Historical Account of Nagaland* spans the history of the various Naga tribes from their ethnological affinities to the outbreak of hostilities and statehood. Hamlet Bareh came up with his doctoral thesis, *History and Culture of the Khasi People*. J.N. Choudhury next presented a more readable *Khasi Canvas.* His other noteable studies *Arunachal Panorama* and *Arunachal Through the Ages* continue to be in demand. A slender book *Tripura Through the Ages* by Nalini R. Choudhury set a trend for projecting the history of that state. Vumson's *Zo History* attempts to broaden and integrate the various clans and tribes of the Zos viering away from the earlier works (by Mizos), who generally make Lushai central to all history of the Mizos. The study by Suhas Chatterjee *Mizoram Under British Rule*, set the pace for later and more detailed histories.

Under the guidance of H.K. Barpujari a team of historians have been working over the years in an ambitious and result oriented *The Comprehensive History of Assam.* Financed by the Publication Board, Assam, the five volume history covers the time span from Pre-history to 1919 and includes the history of the neighbouring hills. The volumes cover the art, religion, social and economic conditions apart from political and administrative developments. A reviewer noted that "old interpretations and conclusions have been re-examined, re-assessed and even revised,"[11] in the background of the tremendous extend of research that is now available. Numismatics has been a core area of research in North East India. Beginning with the interest shown by British collectors a small and closely connected group of numismatists continue to find areas of study and broadening their interpretations to social and economic life. Some notable studies in this field are the essay in J.P. Singh and Nisar Ahmad (ed.) *Coinage and Economy of North Eastern States of India,*[12] J.P. Singh, *Monetary Development in Early Assam,*[13] contributions to the 3rd International Colloquium *Coinage Trade and Economy,*[14] and Nicholas Rhodes, *Coins of North East India* delivered as lectures in the North East Hill University in 1995 under the H.K. Barpujari endowment.[15]

Archaeology and Prehistory continue to draw attention of scholars to explain questions of antiquity. Here again the start made by British officials reporting on archeological finds was then taken by the Archaeological Survey of India undertaking excavations,[16] and scholars individually or collectively working on sites scattered from as far as Malinithan in Arunachal Pradesh to Baitbari in the Garo Hills and the Ambari excavations in Guwahati.[17] Interesting extensions of these disciplines have been done in art history, iconography, and inscriptions. While individual researches of this nature find mention in academic circles it is regretted that the region, including the recent researches in the early history of the Nagas, Khasis and Garos has not found adequate mention in general histories of India. The same seems to be the case with the ancient, medieval and modern history of Assam (the plains areas) where substantial contributions have been made and yet are not given much notice by Indian scholars. The writing of the history of North-East India a historian argues has been overlooked in general histories of India because of the "poverty of material which has an all India bearing," and that "this region has not so far been an inherent part of the historical consciousness of India."[18] It must be admitted that scholars in the region have generally an insular approach. There has been no historian from the region who has written a 'national' history and use of parallels and comparisons from beyond East Bengal have been few. The focus here has generally been region, state, valley and society.

Notwithstanding this approach confined as it is, the thrust and focus of historical inquiry has been drawn to newer areas of research which is both regional and sub-regional as shall be explained. Take state formation for instance. The earlier writings on state formation were largely empirical. The trend today is analytical. Studies in state formation has not been the preserve of historians. Folklorists such as Soumen Sen, *Social and State Formation in Khasi Jaintia Hills*, Delhi, 1985; political scientists as B. Pakem, "State formation in Pre-Colonial Jaintia,"[19] Amalendu Guha's paper on Medieval Assam,[20] and historians with J.B. Bhattacharjee's numerous papers on the subject took up the social, economic and political forces in the state formation of Srihatta, Tripura, Jaintia and Cachar. H.J.M. Claessen and Peter Skalnik (eds.) in *The Early State*[21] set the academicians working in this area to give fresh interpretations. The "maturity this field has attained over the years" was manifested in three papers on state formation in North East India being included in *Tribal Politics and State System in Pre-Colonial and North East India*,[22] and in *Social and Polity*

*Formation in Pre-Colonial North East India; The Barak Valley Experience.*[23] Recent additions to this investigation are those on the Boros, Mizos, Khasis and Nagas by scholars of the North Eastern Hill University.[24] Research is in progress to examine the processes of state formation in Khyrim and Sohra *Himas.*

Another area of research that has drawn social scientist into debate is the emergence, role played by, and the ideology of the middle class. The research in this case too have been scattered over a whole array of journals with interpretations ranging from a literal understanding of the term to fitting studies in a Marxist framework. Important contributions to this have been done by Hiren Gohain,[25] Amalendu Guha,[26] B. Dutta Ray,[27] A.K. Baruah,[28] R.C. Kalita,[29] M. Sharma[30] among others. These discussions have taken as their space the Brahmaputra valley. Perhaps realizing an over-emphasis of this theme on this valley, a start has been made to extend both the framework and interpretation to the tribal societies.

Linked with the rise of the middle class in Assam has been their involvement and leadership in peasant struggles and the response of nationalists to the freedom movement, the history of which has been fairly well researched. An area that is steadily gaining attention is student movements. The pioneering works of Sheila Bora and Meeta Deka in their coverage of student activity between 1905–1972 on Assam[31] and other younger researchers on Meghalaya and Manipur indicates that much more will be forthcoming on this subject; particularly after the tumultous events of the 1980s in Assam and student activism today.

Research continues on various dimensions of British administration in North East India and in its relations with States that had come under indirect administration. These range from studies on British paternalism to details of policy and pattern with special emphasis on the Garos, Nagas, Mizos, the tribes of Meghalaya. A refreshing approach was undertaken by John Parratt and Saroj Parratt in their study of the Anglo-Manipuri conflict of 1891.[32] It was intended to have the book out in the centenary of the events it describes. Whereas this book has been fairly well received another which commented on the same events did not get a cordial reception. While at this it may not be out of place to indicate that often historical research is encouraged by the number of years lapsing after an event. This seminar itself has set the time frame for its discussion to begin in 1947. Surprisingly not much interest was generated on the end of the Second World War and its 50 years retrospect but for a Presidential Address to the Indian History Congress.[33] Even 50 years of India's independence seemed to have little impact among the history community.[34] Need we wait platinum and centenary celebrations?

Church history of North East India has not made a complete break from the 'missionary approach' to mission history. It is understandable why for instance J.H. Morris, C. Becker or V. Sword wrote their histories. That dimension continues to have focus and its worth is the information that has been forthcoming on the various missions, particularly after their management by first, second and later generation believers. Guided by the Church History Association of India that its comprehensive *History of Christianity* should have more social focus, F.S. Downs' contribution to that project and particularly his H.K. Barpujari Endowment Lectures at NEHU 1994[35] have shown new avenues to understand the impact of christianity in the region. While the first histories were largely denomination and remain so a healthy trend is witnessed in a more ecumenical approach as in the recent collection of papers in *Impact of Christianity on North East India*.[36]

With so much written on its history it was expected and desirable that the historiography of North East India would be taken up. The gap in time between the review of Gait's history and the present concern on historiographical issues has been long but more than made up by historians of the region reviewing the developments on the subject.[37] Historigraphical studies, however, have been few and therefore not sufficiently developed to provide a critical but appreciative assessment of the studies that have been undertaken.

The progress of historical research in the region has been made possible in part by the location of the new material, opening of archives and use of material previously not given much attention by historians. Historians have had to carefully venture to other disciplines in the humanities and social sciences to use tools to understand the past. It has been possible for researchers not trained in the discipline to write histories for which there are numerous examples. As new material is located and archival material becomes available fresh studies will be undertaken; details will be added; additional chapters will be incorporated and reinterpretations will be attempted. The historian will be writing side by side with sociologists, political scientists, economists and those of other allied disciplines as was done for *Hill Cities*[38] or for the newer interests in ethnicity, nationalism, oral history, forest and environmental history.[39] Where economists have set a trend in economic history,[40] historian in the interest of their subject and to fill in this serious gap need to broaden their visions.

## REFERENCES


1. George Edward Westmacott, "Description of Ancient Temples and Ruins at Charduar in Assam," *J.A.S.B.*, Vol. IV, 1835, pp. 185–186; and his unpublished and little noticed 7 volume "History of Assam" at King's College Aberdeen University. For details of the manuscript see D.R. Syiemlieh, "Westmacott's History of Assam", *Proceedings of the North East India History Association*, Seventeenth Session, Aizawl, 1996, pp. 94–98.
2. *Report on the Progress of Historical Research in Assam*, Shillong, 1897.
3. *Early British Relations with Assam: A Study of the Assam Records of the East India Company*, Shillong, 1925; *Lachit Barphukan and His Times*, Guwahati, 1947; *Atan Buragohain and His Times. A History of Assam from the Invision of Mir Jumle in 1662-63 to the Termination of Assam Mogul Conflicts in 1682*, Gauhati, 1957; *Anglo-Assamese Relations 1771–1826*, Guwahati, 1949.
4. Cited in Sheila Bora, "Projecting Assam's History and Culture: Dr. S.K. Bhuyan's Mission," pp. 2–5, Paper read at a Colloquium on S.K. Bhuyan at the Fifteen Session of the North East India History Association, Doimukh, 1994.
5. See for instance, the late Subhash Chandra Saha, "Grassroot Nationalism: A Study of Mass Resistance in the District of Darrang and Nowgong 1937–47", unpublished Ph.D. dissertation, NEHU, 1980; Riaz Uddin Ansari, "1942 Movement in Darrang District with special Reference to Dekhiajuli", unpublished M. Phil dissertation, NEHU, 1998, for the type of studies and approaches to Assam's involvement in the nationalist movement. There is much material in Assamese on this subject which the bibliographies of the studies noted above used.
6. Irfan Habib, "The Contribution of Indian Historians to the Process of National Integration", *Proceedings of the Indian History Congress*, 1961, p. 357.

7. Hamlet Bareh, *U. Tirot Singh*, Delhi, 1984.
8. Jerlie Tariang, *Tirot Singh*, New Delhi, 1990.
9. Presidential Address, *Proceedings of the North East India History Association*, First Session, Shillong, 1980, p. 12.
10. K.S. Singh, The Merger of Manipur with India, *Proceedings of the NEIHA, Third Session*, Imphal, 1982, pp. 224–228; K.R.K. Sharma, 'The Merger of Manipur into India: A Brief Note', *Proceedings of the NEIHA*, Fourteenth Session, Jorhat, 1993, pp. 275–277; D.R. Syiemlieh, "The Political Integration of the Khasi State into the Indian Union", B. Pakem (ed.), *Regionalism in India*, NEHU Publications, Shillong, 1995, pp. 147–156. The History Department, Assam University, Silchar, is soon to organise a Seminar on 'Integration'.
11. S.K. Barpujari, "State of Historical Research in North East India", Bi-Decennial Celebration of North-East India Council for Social Sciences Research, 30th June 1994, *Journal of NEICSSR*, pp. 13–14.
12. Memoir No. 7., *The Numismatic Society of India*, Varanasi (n.d.).
13. Asam Sahitya Sabha, Jorhat, 1989.
14. *Indian Institute in Numismatic Research*, 1991.
15. To be published shortly by Harman Pub. House, New Delhi.
16. See, *A Source Book of the Archaeology of Assam and Other States of North Eastern India*, Kamarupa Anusandhan Samiti, Reprinted, 1984.
17. It should not be mistaken that the Malinithan and Baitbari settlements and temple sites had tribal Arunachalis or Garos as their authors for present day boundaries have no relevance in this context. See A.K. Sharma, *Emergence of Early Culture in North East India*, New Delhi, 1993.
18. O.P. Kejariwal, "The North-East in Indian Historiography: The Need for a Corrective", *Proceedings of the North East India History Association*, Fourth Session, Pasighat, 1986, p. 21.
19. *NEHU Journal of Social Sciences and Humanities*, Vol. II, No. 3, 1984.
20. "The Ahom Political System: An Enquiry into the State Formation in Medieval Assam," Occasional Paper CSSS, Calcutta, 1983.
21. The volume included a chapter on the Kachari state by Sofia Marentina who based her research largely on C.A. Soppitt, *A Historical and Descriptive Account of the North Cachar Hills*, Shillong, 1885.
22. J.B. Bhattacharjee, *Social and Polity Formation in Pre-Colonial North East India: The Barak Valley Experience*, New Delhi, 1991. The three papers in the seminar edited by Surajit Sinha were authored by J.B. Bhattacharjee (Cachar), B. Pakem (Jaintia), H. Bareh (Khasi).
23. *Ibid.*
24. R.N. Mochahary, "Social History of the Bodos of Assam", Ph.D. NEHU; R. Buragohain, "Ahom State Formation in Assam", Ph.D. NEHU; V. Bawitlung, "Chieftainship and the Processes of State Formation" in Mizo Society", Ph.D. NEHU, 1998.
25. "Origins of the Assamese Middle Class", *Social Scientist*, No. 3, August, 1973.
26. A. Guha, *op. cit*, pp. 56–64; "Making of the Assamese Middle Class", Paper presented at a seminar on Resource Base and Problems of Regionalism of North Eastern Region of India, NEHU, 1977; "A Big

Push Without a Take Off: a Case of Assam (1871–1902)", *The Indian Economic and Social History Review*, Vol. V, No. 3, 1968.

27. B. Datta Ray (ed.), *The Emergence and Role of Middle Class in North East India*, New Delhi 1983, has 8 papers included in the volume.
28. "Assamese Middle Class and the Xenophobic Tendencies in Assamese Society", *Frontier*, Vol. 14, No. 11. "Some Methodological Issues in the History of the Assamese Middle Class", *Proceedings of the NEIHA*, Fourteenth Session, Jorhat.
29. "Nineteenth Century Peasant Movement and the Assamese Middle Class", *Proceedings of the NEIHA*, Fifteenth Session, Doimukh 1994; "Immigration to Assam: British Policy and Assamese Middle Class (1836–1900), *Proceedings of the NEIHA*, Thirteenth Session, Shillong, 1993.
30. *Social and Economic Changes in Assam: Middle Class Hegemony*, Delhi, 1990; "Peasant Unrest in Nineteenth Century Assam: Peasant Vs. State, Atul Goswami (ed.), *Land Reforms and Peasant Movement*, Guwahati, 1986; "The Assamese Middle Class: Its Role in the 'Peasant Uprisings of 1893-94', in B. Datta Ray (ed.), *op. cit.*
31. Sheila Bora, *Student Revolution in Assam 1917–1947*, N. Delhi, 1992; Meeta Deka, *Perspective of the Years of Student Protest; A Historical Survey in Assam 1905–72*, Ph.D. NEHU, 1995; also Jagat Bora, "Assamese Students and their activities in the Freedom Movement," *Proceedings of the NEIHA*, Fourteenth Session, Jorhat, 1993.
32. J. and S. Parratt, *Queen Empress Vs. Tikendrajit Prince of Manipur*, New Delhi, 1992.
33. J.B. Bhattacharjee, "World War II and India: A Fifty Years Perspective", *Presidential Address, Indian History Congress*, Modern India Section 1989.
34. Some years earlier however, *The Indo-British Review* published a volume on the *Partition of India and Pakistan 1947–1971*, Vol. XVII, No. 1 and 2, September–December 1989 in which the papers of D.R. Syiemlieh, "Response of the North-Eastern Hill Tribes of India Towards Partition and Independence", pp. 27–35, and J.B. Bhattacharjee, "Sylhet: Myth of a Referandum", pp. 37–51, were incorporated.
35. *History of Christianity in India; North East India in the Nineteenth and Twentieth Centuries*, Bangalore, 1992; *The Christian Impact on the Status of Women in North East India*, NEHU, 1996.
36. Edited by J. Pukhenpurakal the book is a collection of 34 papers written by Christians of different denominations. The seminar was jointly organised by the Sacred Heart Theological, Shillong, and the History Department, NEHU, in 1995.
37. Manorama Sharma and J.B. Bhattacharjee, "Historical Research on North East India: Trends and Directions" in T. Banerjee (ed.), *Indian Historical Researches Since Independence*, Calcutta, 1986; S.K. Barpujari, "State of Historical Research in North East India", *Journal of the NEICSSR*, 30th June 1994; and articles by Shrutidev Goswami, Manorama Sharma, S.K. Barpujari in *Proceedings of the NEIHA*, Fourteenth Session, Jorhat, 1993, and by others in various other *Proceedings of NEIHA*.
38. A.C. Sinha et al. (ed.), *Hill Cities of Eastern Himalayas Ethnicity Land Relations and Urbanisation*, N. Delhi, 1992.

39. The Assam University, Silchar, has taken a lead in some of these areas.
40. Amalendu Guha's delightful saving grace, "The Medieval Economy of Assam" as an appendix in Tapan Raychaudhuri and Irfan Habib (eds.), *The Cambridge Economic History of India*, N. Delhi, 1991; Mumammad Abu B. Siddique, *Evolution of Land Grants and Labour Policy of Government; The Growth of the Tea Industry in Assam 1834–1940*, N. Delhi, 1990.

# 4

# Some Trends of Research in Economics in North Eastern India

*N. Srivastav*

The primary objective of this survey is to present major trends of research on some aspects of Economics in North-East India. The efforts are made to cover a time period for about four decades and to put the research work in proper perspective, an inter connected account of the major issues that got attention of the various social scientists from time to time. In particular the attempt is focussed on the developments during last twenty years.

At the outset, it is to be confessed that this survey is neither complete, nor exhaustive and comprehensive, because efforts of an individual researcher, naturally set the limit. More detailed survey of the research work in the field of Economics for entire five decades, calls for vast resources and collective efforts, which are beyond the reach of singular research scholar. Individual efforts can, however, be significant, as in this survey, as an additional source of available information and meant to be an informative source about the state of research in the field of Economics in North-Eastern India.

It is worthwhile to mention that only the published research work in research journals, books and seminar papers published in edited volumes could be included in this paper. The research work undertaken by the various departments of the Universities, research institutions and agencies, which is unpublished is not the part of this survey for obvious reasons.

## Major Trends of Research in Economics

In order to capture the major trends in the various fields of Economics, more than one hundred titles are reviewed. Out of which seventy five studies are selected for the purpose of analysis, on the ground of well defined research problem, scientific methodology and relevant findings. It is assumed that seventy five number of titles form a significantly large sample size and could be considered as a representative sample of the available research work in the region in the field of Economics. On the basis of this assumption, this sample would reflect a bird's eye view of the major trends and status of research in Economics in North Eastern part of India.

Table 1 represents the decomposition of reviewed research work in North Eastern region. Out of total research titles reviewed, books reviewed are 43.6%, articles published in edited volumes constitute 35.9% and articles published in various research journals are 20.5%. It is important to note that a largest volume of research material is available in book form, followed by articles published in edited volumes. The titles are significantly distributed among all the categories. Research articles are mostly published in Economic and Political Weekly, Manpower, Social Action, Indian Journal of Agricultural Economics and other well reputed journals of national standard. These journals are widely circulated in India and abroad, if more research output is getting chance to publish in these and other journals, then more and more social scientists from rest of India would be aware of major economic issues and problems of north eastern part of India. This would lead to attract the due attention among the academicians at large.

The reviewed research literature is also arranged in temporal frequency distribution in decadel form, beginning from 1955–65, 1966–75, 1976–85 and 1995 onwards, according to the respective year of publication. Analysing this time series, it is found that while 8.3% literature is published during the decade 1955–65, in onwards decades this percentage is continuously increasing and reaching the peak during the period 1985–95,

Table 1. Decomposition of research work

| Types | Research in Numbers | Titles in Percentage |
|---|---|---|
| Books | 33 | 43.6 |
| Edited volume | 27 | 35.9 |
| Articles | 15 | 20.5 |
| Total | 75 | 100 |

where 46.6% research work is published (See Table 2). This accelerating growth in research publication is a very encouraging trend, which implies that recently more and more social scientists are paying attention towards the contemporary economic issues of the region. Emergence of new universities, departments and research institutions may certainly be a significant factor in explaining the temporal growth of research publications.

It is expected that this healthy trend will grow in future and provide a positive encouragement to young researchers in the field. Most of the research publication after 1995 must be in pipe line and various stages of publication, which is reflected by the fact that only 5% reviewed research work is available for this period of reference.

North Eastern part of India comprises of heterogeneous geographical regions and inhabitants with diverse culture, religion and of different socio-economic status. This region is sub-divided into seven states for the purpose of civil and political administration. The awareness towards higher education and research is spreading speedily in all the north eastern states. Therefore, the facilities and opportunities are also fast

Table 2. Temporal distribution of research work publication

| Year | Research Work Publication | |
|---|---|---|
| | in numbers | in percentage |
| 1955–65 | 6 | 8.3 |
| 1966–75 | 10 | 13.3 |
| 1976–85 | 20 | 26.7 |
| 1985–95 | 35 | 46.6 |
| 1995– | 4 | 5.0 |
| TOTAL | 75 | 100 |

emerging in this region to meet the supply and demand of skilled and educated manpower. Consequently, it would be interesting to analyse the regional (state-wise) distribution of research output. Table 3 demonstrates the state-wise regional distribution which suggests that a large number of research titles are available in the field of economics, where entire north eastern region is studied as one unit and inter-state comparison are made for the purpose of analysis. On the other hand, some studies are of general nature and not for a region specific. Both of these two types of studies are kept in separate categories in Table 3. Among the seven states largest number of studies are available for the state of Assam (28.0%), followed by Meghalaya (12.0%) and Manipur (6.6%). Least number of reviewed literature available for Mizoram (3.0%) followed by Arunachal Pradesh (4.0%) and Tripura (5.3%). It is worthwhile to mention that availability of research of both has a strong association with the number of active research institutions and university departments in the state.

Table 3. Regional distribution of research work

| Region | Research Work in number | in percentage |
|---|---|---|
| Meghalaya | 9 | 12.0 |
| Assam | 21 | 28.0 |
| Tripura | 4 | 5.3 |
| Arunachal Pradesh | 3 | 4.0 |
| Mizoram | 2 | 3.0 |
| Manipur | 5 | 6.6 |
| Nagaland | 3 | 4.0 |
| NE Area | 21 | 28.0 |
| General | 7 | 9.3 |
| Total | 75 | 100.0 |

Economics as a discipline can also be divided into well-recognised fields of specializations. One may find it interesting to analyse that distribution of research work as field wise in economics (See Table 4). Largest proportion of research output is available (26.3%) in the field of economy and economic development in NE region, followed by rural development and regional planning (18.0%). 16.4 % studies are available from the field of agricultural economics. Relatively speaking,

Table 4. Distribution of research work in various fields of economies

| Field | Research work in | |
|---|---|---|
| | Number | Percentage |
| Agricultural economies | 12 | 16.4 |
| Transport & trade economies | 4 | 4.9 |
| Economy & Development | 20 | 26.3 |
| Education/MPP | 4 | 4.9 |
| Land economies | 10 | 13.1 |
| Rural Dev.& regional planning | 13 | 18.0 |
| Public finance | 1 | 1.61 |
| Production technology | 1 | 1.61 |
| Industrial economics | 4 | 4.9 |
| Planning in NE | 6 | 8.2 |
| Total | 75 | 100 |

lesser amount of studies representing the fields of public finance, taxation, production technology, industrial economics and trade/transport economics. This distribution is not surprising as NE economy is still characterised mainly, as agricultural and rural based economy, with less degree of industrialisation. But it is surprising that this region has vast mineral and forest resources, but the studies relating to resource economics are available only a few in number. This could be tackled as serious research gap, which has vast scope and potential for research in future. In the era of economic reforms and liberalisation at national level, the economies of North East, would also begin to modernize their economic sectors, through industrialisation, so new research fields would hopefully emerge and have relevance in future. For instance, research effects in the fields of infra-structural economics, inter-industrial economics, trade economics, would be helpful in appreciating the regional economic issues and aspirations, problem and perspectives in coming future.

## Emerging Issues in the Field of Research in Economics

It would be in the fitness of things, to give a brief account of major issues in the field of research in economics in north eastern India. For this purpose, the abstract of research problems, methodologies and major findings of some of the research studies are discussed and included in this paper.

Land is one of the major factors of production, especially in the region, which is heavily dominated by primary sector and characteristically similar to an economically backward economy. In such case the distribution patterns of land has strong bearings on the socio-economic status of the people in a society. A number of economists have shown their keen interest in this field and issues related to land use pattern, land relations, land reforms and peasant movements are paid due attention in North Eastern India. In this region, in general land areas can broadly be divided into plain and hill areas. The hill areas predominantly dominated tribals inhabitant regions, where land system is governed by traditions and customs. In the plains and valleys, however, there are established laws, defining the relationship among landowners, tenants and governments properly and systematically.

A brief account of the origin of prevailing Land System in the region is available in Das (1986),[1] along with land reform legislations and progress of land reforms. The distributive pattern of land holding may be helpful in explaining the inequality in the land holding among the small medium and large scale farms. Neog and Bordoloi[2] found in his study that lesser inequality in small farms in the North East region excepting in Tripura and Manipur. It is also observed that the existence of inequality in semi medium and medium farms in Nagaland and Arunachal Pradesh. The Lorenz curve analysis demonstrates decrease in inequality in land distribution in Tripura and increase in Arunachal Pradesh and Meghalaya.

The process of land reform, has always been viewed as a strong instrument for socio-economic transformation of an agrarian society. Existing socio-political system and willingness to implement land reform legislations would, in fact, determine, that to what extent the objective to have more equitable rural society is achieved.

Goswami[3] throws light on some of the possible reasons why land reforms in Assam bound to meet limited success. In an organised agricultural sector, once the prices of farm products become renumerative, industrial and mercantile capital is likely to flow in, in the form of capitalist farming, which would result in further set back to marginal and small farmers, which are at present earning their livelihood by practicing subsistence farming. This problem could be tackled by more practical, fruitful and effective integrated rural development programmes for the targeted groups. But most of such programmes like IRDP and JRY etc. are so far failed to achieve their objective.

The slow progress in the front of land reforms is evident from the fact that farm productivity (of paddy) is continuously declining in Assam. Choudhary[4] observed that unless the small plots of land are reorganised together on cooperative basis free from landlordism. The state of affair is not likely to improve significantly. Sharma[5] discussed problems of land among the plain tribes of Assam. It is opined that insufficiency of agricultural land, share cropping, land alienation and rural indebtness are the major problems in the economic upliftment of these people.

In a study, Saha[6] appraise of structural changes in agricultural holdings in Tripura and found that land reform measures in the shape of land ceiling fixing and distribution of surplus land is not very effective in Tripura because, as such there is very little surplus land available for the purpose. The possible solution of this problem should be sought in intensive cultivation with adopting new and improved agricultural techniques and practices.

In most of the economies of rural areas of North Eastern India, the natural balance between agricultural production and consumption is seen disturbed due to increase in population and process of fast detribalisation. The age old land distribution patterns, which were so long suited to satisfy the local needs are no longer practical and effective to solve present day problems. Manipur could be cited as an example where in some areas, improved irrigation facilities, and adoption of new agricultural techniques/practices — selective agricultural cropping have succeeds to deal with the situation at least in short run, (Sharma).[7]

Due to fast monetisation of traditional societies the process of rapid transformation from traditional system of community ownership to the industrial ownership is emerging in Arunachal Pradesh. Accordingly Agarwal[8] expresses his genuine fear that, with the opening up of the economy of this tribal state with rest of India, the influx of cash flow, a new class of moneyed tribals would emerge. In the absence of alternative investment avenues they would like to purchase land, this would further increase the land holding inequalities in the state in future.

The rapid economic development depends on the rational use of technologies to produce optimum amount of goods and services. This process would in turn generate income, employment opportunities and improve standard of living of the people at large. But, quite often economic benefits of technologies are over-emphasized and its impact on society and long run effects on ecology are either underestimated or totally ignored. Keeping the seriousness of the issue in mind, technology assessment should be given due importance, which could suggest policies to minimise the adverse effects of proposed technology. For this type of assessment the needed statistical information and data have to be processed carefully before arriving at final conclusion. Mohan and Jain[9] suggest that natural resource data management evolved by Department of Science and Technology, Government of India, supplies the required statistical information. In this study an attempt is made to describe the major mineral resources of North Eastern Hill States. Furthermore, some priority industries are identified, which would be economically viable and suitable for the region.

A comparative analysis of land use pattern and land based occupation is made available on decade basis from 1951-52 to 1977-78, by Ganguly.[10] Study, also, presents future projections for the year 2001 AD on the basis of past trends. Certain measures are suggested for long term land use planning for North Eastern region. The need of active role of respective state governments, is emphasized for the purpose of overall economic development.

Age old prevailing institutions play significant role in determining the socio-economic status of the inhabitants in a region. In North-Eastern region, some of the tribal peoples subsist on a primitive mode of 'Slash and Burn' cultivation, more popularly known as shifting (Jhum) cultivation. Such methods of cultivation has been one of the significant factors responsible for soil erosion and destruction of valuable forest resources. State has been trying so wean them from the practice to settle in plains from hill tops and sloppy terrains to adopt permanent plough cultivation. The socio-economic changes of these measures are of great interest and importance. Ganguly[11] presents a systematic enumeration of the economic problems of the 'Jhumias' (cultivators who practice Jhum) of Tripura. This work helps in understanding the 'modus operandi' of Jhuming, as an economic social organisation. Study also highlights the prevailing economic conditions and standard of living of Jhumias. It is opined that the process of conversion of the Jhumias into the settled cultivation should be gradual one, keeping in mind the receptivity, responsiveness and capability to absorb the new and alien system of cultivation from the point of view of Jhumias. State efforts are duly recognised in this regard.

A brief reference is appropriate to an inter-disciplinary study of shifting cultivation in North East India by Ramkrishanan.[12] It is observed that in this region agriculture is closely linked with other sub-systems of village eco-system function and with forestry. So, a holistic approach, which takes into account people's perception of ecology conservation at a human level should be encouraged. The relationship between poverty, deforestation and conservation could be reversed by rural development programmes.

Thus, issues of shifting cultivation is closely related to sustainable development and environment. Control of shifting cultivation is possible by suggesting economically viable and acceptable and practical rural development programmes and encouragement of agro-based activities for an alternative/ additional source of livelihood.

It has been recognised for a long time that environmental disruption is a complex issue, which is interactive in nature and leads to environmental degradation. North Eastern part of India facing a problem of deforestation, Srivastav,[13] estimates forest areas lost for various purposes during 1951-52 to 1975-76 in seven North Eastern States. Assam has highest area lost proportionately, followed by Tripura, Arunachal Pradesh and Nagaland. In Assam large amount of forest area lost due to housing and agricultural purposes to satisfy private and public needs. Need is felt to introduce social indicators, environment assessment programmes auditing in development planning system.

Economic planning is a systematic and coordinated effort on the part of political authority to improve the performance of the economy. A regional economic planning needs to set up targets for various sectors to be achieved in given time frame. The success of planning very much depends upon critical assessment, constant monitoring of the plan performance on the basis of feasibility consistency and optimality studies related to performance of planning in North East have generated in wide spread interest and concern. It is pertinent to consider first the efforts of Dutta,[14] who felt that in the absence of effective local level planning machinery the successive implementation of planning is not possible in Assam. It was further, noticed that lack of commitment of the departmental executives and the un-availability of senior officers of planning departments at sub divisional level are added dimensions for the limited success of micro/local level planning.

To resolve some of these issues, it is necessary to identify the most backward regions in any region and priority may be given to such regions, while distributing the development grants. One such exemplary efforts are made by Deka,[15] where thirty one community development blocks of Meghalaya were put to ranking orders, on the basis of predefined indicators for relative economic backwardness. Further, it is emphasized, that more effective planning is only possible through joint efforts of politicians, planners and executives.

Reference has already been made, to one of the common criticism, about the planning in North East India is lack of local level participation and decentralization. Local level government machinery are not normally involved. In this context Dasgupta,[16] evaluates the role of gram-panchayats in planning in Tripura since 1971, where these panchayats (Gaon Sabha) are entrusted with a key role in rural development schemes implementation. Study concludes that rapid economic development needs a strong and effective planning machinery at all levels, special reference has been made to revitalise community development blocks. Dutta[17] suggests that the planning commission should initiate action to set up a state development council to coordinate the different sub-division planning cells. All the secretaries of sub-divisional level cells should be the members of council. This council should: (i) under take awful-scale survey of resources in various sub-divisions, (ii) take up a land survey with regard to its utilization capabilities, (iii) arrange marketing surplus product in the district level and remove transport bottlenecks, (iv) ensure support and utilisation of local intellectuals and various technical persons available locally, (v) building up entrepreneurship at the local level.

To build up such structure need was felt for a regional planning body for NE region to suggest reforms in techniques of planning, planning strategy best suited for the region. In order to serve this propose North-Eastern Council (NEC) was inaugurated on 7th November 1972. Das[18] discusses the objectives and functioning of NEC. It was expected that it would emerge as a successful consultancy and intregating planning authority. Critical evaluation of the role of NEC may be assessed on the following grounds: (i) assessment of resource potentials, surveys and up to date data base (ii) development of infrastructure (ii) development of agriculture and allied activities (iv) manpower development (v) industrialisation. Agarwal[19] accounts for various developmental activities of NEC and highlighted its limitations since its inception.

Importance of inter-sectoral and inter-regional linkages are highly appreciated in formulating the plan priorities. Input-output techniques are used quite extensively for this purpose at national and regional levels. Barua[20,21] has made an attempt to apply an aggregated input-output coefficient matrix for Assam for the year 1977 (based on prices of 1969), and identify the key sectors for the economy of Assam. It was found that commercial crop sector has the largest single total linkages followed by agro-based industries. This suggests, that in the process of economic development, these sectors will deserve high priority. In this regard role of NEC becomes very prominent, which can play a role of co-ordinator in bringing out a common strategy of development for NEC (Barua).[22]

We turn now to studies, which raise the issues of agriculture in NE region. This sector not only satisfy the basic need of food, but also a provider of livelihood for large size of population. Goswami and Sakia[23] takes issues related to paddy growers of Assam. Strong association is established between total crop output and marketed surplus. But the tribal inhabitant areas face altogether a different type of problems of adoptability and responsiveness towards development activities undertaken by various agencies (Goswami and Saikia).[24] According to Goswami and Gogoi[25] the market prices of farm products are major determination of the cultivation and disposal of crops like paddy and Jute. This is revealed in a case study Nowgaon district of Assam.

Various policy measures are suggested by agriculture scientists and economists to improve the agricultural productivity, factor productivity so that agricultural sector could be transformed from stage of subsistence level to a profit making economic sector. One of such approach is intensive area development approach. A village level plan is prepared by Saikia.[26] The socio-economic organisations and systems which are prevailing for a long time in a society, affects the behavioural pattern of people. This behavior is reflected in the forms of habit, tradition, work culture, customs and other human interactions, such factors are known as institutional factors. Gohain[27] noticed that such factors are more intense and strong in a close society in tribal dominated areas. This study highlights and identifies those institutional factors which work as a deterrent for economic development.

In a subsistence economy, the agricultural sector, hardly produces any surplus, similarly, agricultural income is also determined by low productivity and almost elastic supply of labour. Phukan and Burgohain[28] determined the extent of surplus income in rural areas of Asssam. Two different agricultural practices, prevailing in most of NE region are shifting cultivation, mainly on hill tops and terrace cultivation on hill slope and plains. Borah[29] asserts in evolving the crop patterns under these two types of cultivations in Garo Hills District of Meghalaya. Khound[30,31,32] discusses the various aspects related to agricultural sector in developing economies. For example, what is the role of agriculture, what should be the strategy for the development of agricultural sector? How the income distribution pattern changes and what is their significance in a society which is in the process of transition? Can we quantify the magnitude and nature of underemployment in agricultural sector?

A comprehensive picture of NE economy is very much needed to understand its economic problems. Agarwal[19] tries to fill this gap and provides a voluminous account of the economy of NE India. It covers natural and human resources and infrastructural development and growth patterns of state domestic products and employment. The role of North Eastern Council is also examined in the context of regional planning. Development aspects related to agriculture and industries are also highlighted. Accordingly, the major economic problems of the region are: inadequate infrastructure, indigenous entrepreneurship, public and private enterprises, dominated by traditional agriculture, non availability of skilled manpower, institutional finance, hostile attitudes of rebels, influx of migrants. Besides, these, difficult terrain, narrow link with the rest of the country further hamper the process of economic growth. The possible and practical remedial measures are also suggested.

In another study at state level about Nagaland, Saleh[33] narrated the major change in the state economy since 1964, structural changes are derived on the basis of inter sectoral changes. It is observed that significant changes are taking place in the economy, which was initially a traditional economy (at the time of statehood in 1963) has slowly moved into stage of nearing 'precondition for take-off'. Further, certain distinctive features are present in the economy of Nagaland like favourable land-men ratio, very low land less peasantry, people's strong faith in dignity of labour, social, spiritual values. These positive indicators may help to lead the economy of state to the path of rapid economic development.

State level study in case of Assam goes date back to 1962, when Goswami[34] included the various aspects of state economy in his work and threw light on the level, magnitude and direction of the economic development of Assam.

More recently, Barua[35] studies industries, infra-structure and state level planning efforts in Assam. It is found that drastic changes are taking place in household demands, thereby, leading to decline of traditional and handloom industries of Assam. Small scale industries find difficulty in marketing their products at sustainable profit rates. Industrial Development Bank of India (IDBI) and North Eastern Council

(NEC) are launching programmes of entrepreneur development but should also give emphasis on follow-up plans and post training situations. Besides this study recommends for thrust area for rapid economic development in fields of infrastructure, finance, marketing and industries.

Discussing the development strategy for the north eastern region, Pathak[36] is of the view that, strategy has to be based on efficient utilisation of its vast untapped natural resources and favoured symbiotic relation between manpower and nature.

To examine the role of industry in economic development of NE India Neog[37] estimated the interdependence of the regional and national economy. To accelerate the growth the resource based model of industrialisation is suggested. To tackle the problems of market constraint development of ancillaries and auxiliaries is strategically viable, provided break even point is with in 50 percent. Baishya[38] presents a case study of small and cottage industries in Kamrup, Barpeta and Nalbari districts of Assam. A diagnostic study based on primary survey of the twenty six small and cottage industries in five sample villages, having high concentration of village industries, appraising critically, analysis highlights the problems of modernisation of village industries and suggests the remedial measures.

Markets are the centres of exchanges where buyers and sellers meet for economic transaction. The markets in rural areas, serves the purpose of selling agricultural produce and enable the farming population to make economic gains. In actual practice, most of the rural markets are dominated by the traders, 'middlemen', who siphoned-off much more from farm producers also, the general view of rural economics of North Eastern India.

There is an urgent need to realise the importance of agricultural market in NE region according to Dasgupta.[39] Much of the problems of rural market are due to communication gap and lack of information, which can be tackled by introducing market intelligence service. With the development of infrastructural facilities and mass media communications the most of the tribal economies are, already passing through a transition state. Nair[40] captured the relevant issues of the economy of the state of Meghalaya. In an inter-temporal analysis, based on extensive field survey, an attempt is made to ascertain the major changes in land tenure system, pattern of its distribution and use. Efforts are made, Burbanroy,[41] date back to 1961 to prepare the socio-economic and demographic profiles of hill areas of NE India on the basis of data provided by census of India. But, this analysis is at very introductory level and prepare the foundation for more detailed analysis. One such effort is available with Sri Prakash,[42] where attempts are made to evaluate the level of economic development of the region on the basis of changes in state domestic products and per capita income. Major findings are: that growth of output has just sufficed to maintain the regional economy on its low income equilibrium levels. It implies, that the regional economies are still trapped in low income equilibrium vicious circle. The most of the developmental efforts are dissipated by increasing rate of growth of population and rise in prices. In a large number of economic sectors production functions are operating at diminishing returns to scale, which needed induction of new technology of production and diversification of product mix more favourable to prevailing local conditions.

Development of human resources, is considered one of the primary condition for rapid economic growth. For this, purpose, it is required to have a detailed assessment of quality and quantity of human resources available and could be mobilise with the help of appropriate efforts. Singh,[43] on the basis of 1981 census developed a composite index of density and growth of population, percentage of non-tribal population, literacy, urbanisation, proportion of people living in large villages and non agricultural workers. Further, the grouping of the composite index in to quartiles bring out four levels of human resources. It is found that plain districts have high to very high level of human resources, while hill districts have low & very low level of human resources. The reason as a whole has a low level of urbanisation. Similarly, analysing the composite index of amenities and human resources, it is observed that two-third of the population of Assam Valley, three-tenth of Cachar, one-fourth of Manipur, four-fifth of Meghalaya, two-third of Nagaland, three-fourth of Tripura, three-fifth of Arunachal Pradesh and four-fifth of Mizoram have low and very low of infrastructure and social amenities.

Rapid economic development needs a strong and effective planning machinery at all levels. Special reference has been made to revitalise community development blocks.

Lawma[44] made an attempt to explain the functioning of labour markets in general and the markets for the educational manpower, particularly in NE region. With the help of levels and types of education, occupation and various sectors of the economy, the patterns between inter and intra regional migrants are also established.

Transport sector is a major component of economic infrastructure. This has direct, indirect and induced effect over the economic development of a region. Medhi[45] analyses the emergence of railway sector and it's impact on the economic development of Assam. It is found that the direct impact on the economy was through reduced cost of transportation, while indirect impact is in the form of forward and backward linkages. Expansion of market (for tea, oil, timber, jute etc.) and growth of some ancillary and auxiliary industries (such as saw mills, brick works, workshops and railway alignment activities) would generate employment and income generation opportunities, in short as well as in long run. Taking full advantage of railway net work, can increase Assam's production potential substantially.

Bhuyan[46] touches the major issues of fiscal economics of Assam. Besides the budgets of the state government, the analysis is also available for the growth of sectoral revenues and expenditures along with major trends and fluctuations. The changes in the pattern of shared taxes and central grants of first seven finance commission are the part of the study. On taxation in Assam, Dass[47] found that the state has high dependency on federal grants and low and declining share of tax devoluation. Further, it has relatively small share of own tax and non-tax revenue. the inter-sectoral, inter-expenditure class and intra-sectoral equity of tax burden is also estimated. It is concluded that there is a considerable scope for raising tax revenue, if tax reform measures are implemented to the tax potential. Mishra & Roy[48] undertakes a sensitive issue of rural indebtness in tribal society and revealed that small and medium size farmers are more in debt than big and marginal farmers. The per capita productive usage of loan and educational levels of the farmers are the major factors to explain the rural indebtness. As a policy measure, it is suggested that institutional provision of loan at easier term may help greatly in rescuing the rural people and peasantry from the clutches of local money lenders.

Various poverty alleviation programmes are running in North Eastern states, but most of the time governmental agencies depend upon the state level aggregated statistics and ignores the inter-district/interblock/intervillage deviations in poverty incidence levels. Srivastav[49] critically evaluates the operation of IRDP in state Meghalaya. Study is based on extensive field survey and throws light on post-implementation effects on rural beneficiaries of this scheme. Lalwani and Thomas[50] in an empirical study based upon the village levels estimate the incidence of poverty in Meghalaya. It is opined that disaggregated poverty estimates at block and village level would give a better understanding and could be used as an instrument for more effective implementation of poverty alleviation programmes.

With the implementation of rural development programme a systematic and regular monitoring and investigation by an independent agency would be helpful in evaluating the degree of success of such programmes according to Lalwani and Thomas.[51] Study reveals that the blocks which have higher incidence of unemployment and poverty have received lesser coverage of JRY in Meghalaya. Under this scheme as an average worker got employment barely of three days in a month at the wage rate of Rs. 22 per day, which is much lower than prevailing market wage rate. Such findings pose serious debates on the implementation of such programmes.

National Rural Employment Programme is another scheme active to alleviate the poverty in the state of Meghalaya. Emphasis of this scheme is laid down to maximize short term and long term employment opportunities. Thomas and Lalwani[52] found that the percentage coverages of villages in Meghalaya is lowest in country barring Arunachal Pradesh in year 1987-88. Inter-temporal and inter-state comparisons are available in Lalwani,[53] where land productivity is estimated on the basis of yield per hectare for cereals, crop-wise for NE states. Strong association is found in declining in rural per capita income and fall in net sown area. Further, the high proportion of cultivators in states total work force could be explained by low economic growth in this region to some extent.

*Further Research*: Research is a continuous process, where by using of scientific techniques, disaggregated data, appropriate statistical techniques there is always a scope of improvement. Nevertheless, some of the areas may be suggested for proper attention in future:

(i) Female participation and their role in economic development could be very relevant and crucial. Interstate and interdistrict differences in female participation rates according to tribe/caste status. Relationship between house hold income and female participation, may be ascertained.

(ii) Problem of chronic unemployment among educated rural/urban youths, their status and interaction with other economic/non economic sectors.

(iii) Determinants of agricultural performance and possible role of new technology in this sector.

(iv) Identify and quantify; the tangible and intangible benefits of formal/non-formal education.

(v) Impact of education on agricultural productivity; whether and in what manner education is one of the significant determinants in the adoption of improved technology and practice, is an important question.

(vi) Studies emphasise on theoretical aspects and supporting empirical investigation of public policies like health, communication, transport and power.

(vii) Regional differences of pricing of essential commodities at rural and urban area, the price determination mechanism and its adjustment in the context of prevailing local conditions.

## REFERENCES

1. Das, J.N., 1996. Land, land relations and land reforms in the plain and valley's of NE India, in Land reforms and peasant movement: A study of NE India, ed. Goswami, A., Omson Publication, Guwahati.
2. Neog, A.N. and Bordoloi, G., 1996 Distributive pattern of land holding & planned agricultural development in NE region of India in Land reforms and peasant movement: A study of NE India, ed. Goswami, A., Omson Publication, Guwahati.

3. Goswami, A., 1996. Land reforms in Assam : A critical review, in land reforms and peasant movement: A study of NE India, ed. Goswami, A., Omson Publication, Guwahati.
4. Choudhury R.K., 1996. Agrarian land reforms measures in Assam : How close are they to allocational and distributional optima in land reforms and peasant movement: A study of NE India, ed. Goswami, A., Omson Publication, Guwahati.
5. Sharma Thakur, G.C., 1996. Problems of land among the plain tribes of Assam in land reforms and peasant movement: A study of NE India, ed. Goswami, A., Omson Publication, Guwahati.
6. Saha, A., 1996. Structural changes in the agriculture in Tripura: some implications in land reforms and peasant movement: A study of NE India, ed. Goswami, A., Omson Publication, Guwahati, 1996.
7. Sharma, D.S., 1996. Land use pattern in Manipur: Intensification called for in land reforms and, peasant movement: A study of NE India, ed. Goswami, A., Omson Publication, Guwahati.
8. Agarwal, A.K., 1996. Changing picture of agrarian relation in Arunachal Pradesh in land reforms and peasant movement: A study of NE India, ed. Goswami, A., Omson Publication, Guwahati.
9. Mohan, S. & Jain A., 1996. Technology for development: The case of the north eastern hill states, in land reforms and peasant movement : A study of NE India, ed. Goswami, A., Omson Publication, Guwahati.
10. Ganguly, J.B., Comparative analysis of land use and land based occupation, in Land reforms and peasant movement: A study of NE India, ed. Goswami, A., Omson Publication, Guwahati.
11. Ganguly, J.B., 1969. Economic problems of the Jhumias of Tripura: A socio-economic study of the system of shifting cultivation in transition, Book Land Pvt. Ltd., Calcutta.
12. Ramkrishnan, P.S., 1992. Shifting agriculture and sustainable development: An inter-disciplinary study from North East India, Man and Biosphere series, Vol. 10, The Parthenon Publishing group, UNESCO, Paris.
13. Srivastav, N., 1990. The Problems, causes of environmental disruption & its political economy, Rajasthan Economic Journal, Vol. 14, No. 1.
14. Dutta K.C., 1985. Need for local level planning for economic development: A case study of Sib-Sagar sub-division, in land reforms and peasant movement: A study of NE India, ed. Goswami, A., Omson Publication, Guwahati, 1996; in planning in North East India ed. K. Alam, Omson Publication, Gauhati.
15. Deka, P., 1996. Areas of need in Meghalaya: A spatial approach to micro level planning in land reforms and peasant movement: A study of NE India, ed. Goswami, A., Omson Publication, Guwahati.
16. Dasgupta, M., 1996. Panchayat Level Planning in Tripura in Land reforms and peasant movement: A study of NE India, ed. Goswami, A., Omson Publication, Guwahati,
17. Singh, J.P., 1982. Human Resources of North East India, Inter India Publications, New Delhi.
17(a). Dutta K.C., F.No. 14
18. Das, S.K. Regional Planning in NE India: The Role of North Eastern Council.

19. Agarwal, A.K., 1997. Economic Problems and Planning in NE India, Sterling Publishers, New Delhi.
20. Barua, S., 1997. Input output Co-efficient matrix· for Assam: An approximation, NE Economic Review, Vol. 1 No. 3.
21. Barua, S., 1997. The identification of Key sectors in the economy of Assam, NE Economic Review, Vol. 1, No. 3.
22. Barua, S., Certain Observations on the Strategy of development of the NE Region.
23. Goswami, P.C., and Saikia, P.D., 1968. Disposal of Paddy by surplus Growers: A Study in Assam, Economics and Political Weekly, Vol. III., No. 24.
24. Goswami, P.C., and Saikia, P.D., 1970. Problems of Agricultural Development in Tribal areas: Indian Journal of Agricultural Economics, Vol. XXV, No. 3.
25. Goswami, P.C., and Saikia, P.D., and Gogoi, J., 1965. Effects of prices on cultivation and Disposal of Paddy and Jute: A case study in Nowgaon District of Assam, Indian Journal of Agricultural Economics, Vol. XXVI, No. 4.
26. Saikia, P.D., 1965. Intensive Areas Development Approach: A village level plan for agricultural development, Indian Journal of Agricultural Economics, Vol. XXI, No. 4, Oct–Dec.
27. Gohain, D., 1970. Institutional Factors as Deterrant for Economic Development in Tribal Areas, Indian Journal of Agricultural Economics Vol. XXV.
28. Phukan, U., and Borgohain, D.K., 1972. The study on surplus Income in Rural Areas: A Study in Assam, Indian Journal of Agricultural Economics, Vol. XVIII.
29. Borah, D., 1979. Pattern of Crop Production under shifting and terrace cultivation: A Case Study in Garo Hills, Indian Journal of Agricultural Economics, Vol. XXXIII, No. 4.
30. Khound H.P., 1967. Role of agriculture and strategy for agricultural development in over populated countries. Indian Journal of agricultural economics, Vol. XXIII.
31. Khound H.P., 1970. Changes in Income Distribution pattern and their significance in a society in transition, Indian Journal of Agricultural economics Indian Journal of agricultural economics.
32. Khound H.P., 1974. Towards Measuring Under Employment in agriculture. Indian Journal of Agricultural Economics.
33. Saleh, S.I., Nagaland economy in transition since 1964 Omsons Publications, Guwahati.
34. Goswami, P.C., 1962. The Economic Development of Assam, Guwahati.
35. Barua, P.C., 1992. Planning and Development of Assam, Mittal Publications, New Delhi.
36. Pathak, C.R., Development Strategy in NE Region: Some suggestions in Profile of a development strategy for India's north east ed. Thakur, P., Span Publication Pvt. Ltd., Calcutta.
37. Neog, A.K., Role of industry in economic development of NE India: Projections for 2000 A.D. F. No. 36.
38. Baishya, P., 1989. Small and Cottage industries: A Case Study in Assam, Manas Publications, Delhi.

39. Dasgupta, 1984. Importance of agricultural market intelligence services in NE region, in marketing in NE India: Problems of Rural Market ed. Ganguly, J.B., Omsons Publications, Guwahati.
40. Nair, M.K.S., 1986. Tribal economy in transition : A study of Meghalaya, Inter India Publications, Delhi.
41. Burman Roy, B.K., 1961. Demographic and Socio-economic Profiles of Hill Areas of NE India, Census of India.
42. Sri Prakash, 1987. Development of the economy of NE India: Current status, in Emerging patterns of NE Economy, ed., Mahajan, V.S., Deep and Deep Publications, Delhi.
43. Singh, J.P., 1982. Human Resources of NE India, Inter India Publications, New Delhi.
44. Lawma, T., 1990. Market imperfections and Manpower Planning Common-Wealth Publishers, New Delhi.
45. Medhi, S.B., 1978. Transport system and economic development in Assam, Publication Board, Assam.
46. Bhuyan, P.K., 1984. The regional fiscal economics of Assam, Chugh Publications, Allahabad.
47. Das, S.K., 1987. Dynamics of taxation in a Developing Economy.
48. Mishra, S.K. and Roy, D., 1985. Some observations on rural indebtness: A Case study of four tribal villages of North Lakhimpur sub-division, Assam, Rajasthan Economic Journal, 9(2).
49. Srivastav, N., 1990. IRDP in rural Meghalaya: a critical evaluation, in Hill area developments, issues and perspective, ed. Rai, et-al. Ravat Publications, Jaipur.
50. Lalwani, M., and Thomas, E.D., 1997. Incidence of Poverty in Meghalaya villages, Man and Development.
51. Lalwani, M., and Thomas, E.D., (forthcoming) 1998. Incidence of Poverty among beneficiary house holds and employment generation under JRY: A Case Study of Meghalaya, Economic and Political Weekly.
52. Thomas, E.D., and Lalwani, M.L., April-June. 1997. Meghalaya's experience with NREP, Manpower.
53. Lalwani, M.L., April-June, 1992. Land Productivity in NE India, Social Action, Vol. 42, No. 2.

# 5

# From Folklore to Folkloristics: Growth of Folklore Studies in North-East India 1947–1997

*Soumen Sen*

Although folklore as an academic discipline has long since been established in the university system in the West, our attempts in this direction are only recent. Even a new name, Folkloristics, following the suggestion of Alan Dundes (1965), has been given to the discipline distinguishing it from the material it studies, i.e. folklore. However, we still persist in our country with the old and known term. Folklore is viewed as a mass of material that constitutes a part of our culture which is to be studied not as knowledge *per se* but to bring into bold relief the richness of the culture that helps to augment the sense of national pride. It did not receive the attention it deserved at the academic level. Only in 1981, the University Grants Commission (UGC) thought of initiating a process of introducing folklore in the curricula of Indian Universities and constituted a committee. This committee recommended the establishment of departments and centres of studies in Indian Universities with inter-disciplinary research targets from a social science angle for a systematic study of folklore and teaching programmes upto M.Phil. level.[1] The UGC accepted the recommendations and advised the Universities in 1982 to open departments and centres. Many a universities in the country implemented the UGC recommendation. In North-East India, the Department of Folklore Research of Gauhati University, which was already in existence was strengthened with the introduction of M.Phil. programme in 1984. In the same year North-Eastern Hill University established its Centre for Literary and Cultural Studies with the objective of research and study in the folk cultural heritage of the region. The centre also teaches a Post-Graduate Diploma Course and one optional course in Folkloristics in the M.Phil. programme in the School of Social Sciences. Manipur University has also taken projects and schemes for folklore studies.

The Post-Independence period has three distinct phases of folklore research in North-East India. The first phase upto the sixties can be taken as the phase of continuation of the earlier phase of collection and documentation with an academic thrust. The second is the beginning of the academic era of research and the third, which has a history of about two decades, can be taken as the phase of the growth of the discipline of folkloristics with emphasis on teaching, application of folkloric methodologies and inter-disciplinary approach in research through extensive fieldwork.

The pre-independence period was marked by a nationalistic spirit, a pan-Indian phenomenon. In India, attention to folklore has a history of almost two centuries. It began with the Indologists, followed by the Christian missionaries and colonial administrators. The Indian efforts started in the early part of this century along with the growth of the national movements. The academic era began after independence.

It cannot be denied that folklore studies began in India with the coming of the British. Indology, as a western interest, landed on the country of its concern and the scholars, missionaries and adminstrators started both field collection and study. These materials were mostly used to 'know' the hitherto unknown and 'mysterious' country. With the founding of Royal Asiatic Society, the British Orientalists were encouraged to study Indian tradition. There were also attempts to know the 'unlettered' aspects of Indian culture. It was, however, due to the efforts of Rev. William Carey that more attention was placed on the 'unlettered' aspects and the folkways of life of rural India. After the 'Sepoy Rebellion', the British administration felt the urgent need of studying the life of the ruled people.

The British officers were asked to learn the language of the people and know their cultural heritage which could not be done without a recourse to oral tradition.

In North-East India, the monographs on the different communities written by British officers and published in the latter part of the last and the early part of this century were exemplary works on the descriptive studies of the folkways of life of the peoples and contained translations of the narrative genres of folklore. These have substantially contributed to the growth of folklore studies in North-East India.

Following the Indological-missionary phase of folklore studies including the works of the British administrators stationed in India, came the nationalistic phase. Indian scholars also attempted to produce scientific works. Prominent among them were the early group of Indian anthropologists, historians and literateurs. But the nationalistic trend in folklore scholarship began to consolidate under the encouragement of national leaders. With a surge of nationalistic movement and with the emergence of a new and transformed strand of thought, Indian folklore scholarship got its momentum. The emerging Indian leadership realised that any nationalistic agenda had to be grounded in the tradition and the cultural climate of a nation. However, this nationalistic strand did never ignore the fact of regional variations. Though there has always been an attempt at a sort of synthesis to cultivate an 'Indianness' to accelerate the process of nation building, the folkways remained and bound to have remained distinct in different regions. While realising the potential of folklore in helping the growth of nationalist spirit, attention had to be placed on the tradition of a particular linguistic-cultural group. In North-East India, the location of these efforts, was mainly Assam. Great writers like Lakshinath Bezbarua had taken the lead for collection and publication of different genres of folklore to enhance a sense of identity among Assamese people. That such an awareness of identity and national pride of an ethnic group can be restored through folklore is exemplified by the Seng Khasi in Khasi-Jaintia Hills. The Seng Khasi movement leaders had published, since the beginning of this century, a number of volumes on Khasi religion, customs and other genres of folklore to restore, in their own words, 'faith in traditional culture and religion in the face of a challenge posed by large-scale conversion by Christian missions and denigration of their culture by colonial administrators and missionaries.'[2]

The early part of the post-independence period reflects a continuation of this nationalistic phase and an emphasis has been given, both at the academic and administrative level, on a cultural awareness as a part of the agenda of nation building. National academies, Research Institutes, Archives etc. were established. As an offshoot of these programmes folklore studies received a momentum since, in Indian context, cultural awareness needed to have its root in oral tradition.

North-East India has, perhaps, a place of pride in this scenario because it is here in this region folklore was included in the research agenda of a University as early as in 1955. Gauhati University, still an infant University, started a folklore programme initially with the establishment of an archive and then upgrading it to a Department of Tribal Culture and Folklore Research at the initiative of Professor Birinchi Kumar Barua. An account of this early initiative and the growth of the Department of Folklore Research of Gauhati University has been given by Professor Birendranath Datta which I quote, 'Thanks to his (Professor Barua's) vision and zeal, folklore studies came to be accepted as a discipline worthy of being pursued at the highest academic level at a time that was remarkably early not only for this region but for the country as a whole. It is astonishing how he had forged international connections in the field of folklore studies even before the establishment of Gauhati University in 1948. This is borne out by the manner in which he was associated with the preparation of the famous book *Selected Papers on Folklore* by C.N. Von Sydow published from Copenhagen in 1948. The name of B.K. Barua, Guwahati, Assam, appears conspicuously among those of six scholars drawn from different countries, including the great Stith Thompson, under whose supervision the papers were selected and edited by Lauris Bodker. Barua was then teaching at Cotton College . . . It was at Dr. B.K. Barua's initiative that a programme of folklore studies was started at Gauhati University as early as in 1955. Initially the scheme was for a Folklore Archive which was later upgraded to that of Tribal Culture and Folklore Research. The work of the scheme was looked after by Dr. Barua himself until his death in 1963. In the meantime, he had been to Indiana University at Bloomington, USA as a visiting Professor in Folklore and received a fresh dose of international exposure in the field of folkloristics. The evidence of the extended sweep of his international connections are borne by Vol. No. XV of the *Journal of the Assam Research Society* (1963) which he edited . . . It may be mentioned here that Dr. Barua's *Asamar Loka-Samskriti,* a substantial work in Assamese on the folk culture of Assam, received the Sahitya Akedemi award. If the beginning was made by Dr. Birinchi Kumar Barua, it was left to Dr. Paraphulladatta Goswami to give folklore studies a solid basis as a University discipline . . . Dr. Goswami's doctoral thesis *Assamese Folklore* (1953) . . . was one of the earliest such works in India that had completely made use of the latest theoretical and methodological advances made in the field of the scientific study of folklore . . . . Dr. Goswami took over charge of the scheme of Tribal Culture and Folklore Research at Gauhati University in 1963. He went to Indiana University in the USA as a Visiting Professor and came back with fresh stimuli. In 1972, the fullfledged Department of Folklore Research was established at Gauhati University with support from the University Grants Commission — perhaps the first independent department in the country concerned exclusively with folklore studies. And to Dr. Goswami went the distinction of holding the first ever chair of Professor of Folklore in the country . . . . Thanks to the foresight and dedicated services of these pioneers, folklore as an academic discipline has taken roots in the north-east' (Datta 1993).

That was the beginning of the academic era of folklore studies in North-East India. Since then there has been a steady growth and spread of Folkloristics as an academic discipline in the University system. Gauhati University introduced Ph.D. programme in 1972 and M.Phil. programme in 1984. Manipur University also started Ph.D. programme and regular folklore research in the Department of Manipuri. Folklore contents also feature in the M.A. and Degree Major Courses in Assamese of Gauhati and Dibrugarh Universities. North-Eastern Hill University, by establishing the Centre for Literary and Cultural Studies in 1984, has undertaken folklore research as a major component of its programme and started teaching a one-year Post Graduate Diploma Course and an extra-departmental Course in Folkloristics in the M.Phil. programme in the School of Social Sciences. Very recently, three newly established Universities in the region have also placed emphasis on folklore studies. Folklore is a major component in the M.A. and M.Phil. courses in the Department of Tribal Studies of Arunachal University, in the modular course from Certificate to M.A. in the Department of Traditional Culture and Art Forms of Tezpur University. Assam University has folklore in its M.A. Course in Bengali and is planning to establish a Centre in the Department for an advanced research in Folklore. Department of Traditional Culture and Art Forms, Tezpur University and the Centre for Literary and Cultural Studies, North-Eastern Hill University have planned folklore research and archival programme in a big way with the assistance from the Ford Foundation.

Outside the University system, folklore scholarship in the North-East received a distinct direction in the research wing of the North-East Frontier Agency administration (presently Arunachal Pradesh) under the guidance of Verrier Elwin. His own books are highly esteemed works on folklore of the region. But the most significant contribution that Elwin has made is his inspiring leadership in research based on sustained fieldwork with intimate knowledge of the folkways of life of the peoples. This has been a model for research, particularly in the tribal areas, initiated by other agencies in the North-East. In the post independence period Tribal Research Institutes at the state and district levels were established in Assam (before reorganization), Tripura and Manipur. These institutes had also the programmes of collection, documentation and publication of folklore material. The North-Eastern Regional Centre of the Anthropological Survey of India has also done some work. The recently established Anundooram Borooah Institute of Language, Art and Culture, Assam has also folklore research in its agenda. But it must be admitted that these efforts suffered from an absence of appropriate theoretical and methodological framework required for folklore research.

This is a major deficiency in folklore scholarship not only in the North-East but in other parts of the country as well. This is due to a lack of adequate orientation in folkloric methodology and absence of appropriate theoretical framework. Though in recent years there has been a wind of change, much still needs to be done by upholding the claim of Folkloristics as a distinct discipline in the academic system. Otherwise, folklore scholarship will continue to be amaeturish and non-professional. As the UGC Committee (1982) has observed, 'even the collections of folklore material that are at present available are seriously inadequate and uneven. Inadequacies in the procedure of analysis and interpretation of folklore data have also resulted in many vital gaps and distortions'. This is due to the non-professional approach still pursued by folklore scholars. Since folklore is a communicative system based on folk cognition involving social interaction, much needs to be done from the social science angle. All the folklore genres engulf within themselves socially defined communicative situations.

In North-East India there has been, in the post independence period, a welcome approach in social science research for an inter-disciplinary thrust. It has been realised, rightly so, that research in this region, with a conglomeration of peoples with diverse cultural heritage and identity, needs to cross the boundaries of conventional disciplines. A look at the research programmes, Ph.D. and M.Phil. titles in at least one University (North-Eastern Hill University) I am aware of, provides evidences of such an approach. And, these research schemes, particularly those dealing with tribal situations, have drawn, to a large extent, from oral sources.

One example: the historians of this region believe that the frontiers of the discipline called History need to be expanded and there should be schemes for writing regional history, particularly ethno-history, drawing material largely from oral sources. In two presidential addresses in the annual sessions of North-East India History Association, Professor J.B. Bhattacharjee and Professor J.P. Singh have emphasized the utility of folklore material in writing such history (Bhattacharjee, 1992; Singh, 1996). There has been a suggestion as well to use folkloric methodologies in unfolding social dynamics behind an oral tradition and an historian can fruitfully utilise both folkloric and historical methodology. This makes the concern of the historian and the folklorist identical (Bhattacharjee, 1992).

With this importance of folklore realised in social science circle with a similar realisation in folklore circle for more and more inter-disciplinary interaction, Folkloristics, as a distinct discipline, gains momentum. Much now depends upon professional folklorists and academic administrators to put it to its legitimate place. In the process the world of knowledge will expand and social engineering will be strengthened.

## ENDNOTES

1. The Committee's Report, circulated to the Universities in 1982, says, 'In most of the regions of our country the study of folklore was pioneered by scholars of languages and literature. These studies brought into bold relief the richness of the culture and helped to augment the sense of national pride which was so necessary during the days of struggle foe independence. But from a social angle much needs to be done. Even the collections of folklore material that are at present available are seriously inadequate and uneven . . . . Inadequacies in the procedure of analysis and interpretation of folklore data have also resulted in many vital gaps and distortions (UGC Report 1982). The Committee felt that unless attempts are made to introduce Folklore as a discipline in the Universities in the country these gaps and distortions cannot be removed. They therefore recommended opening of departments and centres of studies in Indian Universities.
2. For a detailed discussion, see my papers 1991 and 1994.

## REFERENCES

Bhattarchajee, J.B. 1992 'North-East Indian Perspectives in History' *Presidential Address, XIV Annual Session, North-East India History Association.*

Datta, Birendranath 1993 'Folklore Studies and the North-East', *Journal of NEICSSR,* Vol. 17. No. 1.

Dundes, Alan 1965. 'What is Folklore' (in) *The Study of Folklore* Ed. Alan Dundes. New Jersey: Englewood Cliffs.

Sen, Soumen 1991 'Status of Folklore Studies in North-East India', *Proceedings of North-East India History Association* 12th Session, Shillong: NEIHA. 1994 'Folklore Research in North-East India', *Journal of NEICSSR,* Bi-Decennial Celebration Number-

Singh, J.P. 1996 'Swan-Maiden or The Folk Literature of Tribal North-East India and Buddhist Sudhana Kumaravadanam' *Presidential Address, XVII Annual Session, North-East India History Association.*

UGC Committee 1982 *Report on the Promotion of Folklore Studies.*

6

# Emerging Trends in Philosophy: North-East India Scenario

*S.C. Daniel*

The paper is an attempt to bring out the emerging trends in philosophy in North-East India. In order to do this, it is imperative on my part to define what philosophy is. Therefore, I would like to give a working definition of philosophy before I try to focus on the emerging trends in philosophy in the North-Eastern part of our country.

It is a perennial source of embarrassment for a philosopher like me to be asked to define 'philosophy'. The definition of philosophy has itself become a vexing problem in philosophy. Duscasse says: "What subject matter is peculiar to philosophy, what questions about it are philosophical, what method is appropriate to the solving of them. . . . What philosophy contributes to the life of man — all these are genuinely philosophical questions. They belong to a branch of inquiry which, although it is seldom explicitly included in the lists of philosophical disciplines, is unquestionably one of them. This discipline is the philosophy of philosophy."[1]

Different philosophers have variously defined the nature of philosophy. There is no agreement among the philosophers as to what philosophy is. This disagreement arises because philosophers think about every thing, including philosophy. Indeed, philosophers are delighted by their disagreement; they agree to disagree. There are other reasons as well, which make it difficult to provide a universal 'definition', or a definition which is acceptable to all, of philosophy. Philosophy is a subject that is open ended, and it is concerned with an immense variety of things. Its interests change frequently, and philosophers of different cultural mileus have taken diverse interests in the many divisions of the 'field'. However, it is rather misleading to speak of philosophy as a 'subject' or 'field' for, philosophy is not a fixed body of knowledge or a given set of problems. Philosophy is the *activity of philosophizing*. It is a game, and like in a game, the activity of philosophizing is governed by certain rules. According to Walter Kaufmann, philosophy subverts man's satisfaction with himself, exposes custom as a questionable dream, and offers not so much solution as a different life. What philosophy meant to Socrates has long been considered as one of the most impressive of all statements about philosophy. Because Socrates completely embodied the spirit and pursuit of philosophy. So much so, his explanation of his life and activities is itself an explanation of philosophy. Philosophy, for Socrates, was the quest, the eternal search for wisdom. For him, to be wise meant to be good. It is no wonder, therefore, Plato, his student and torch bearer of his philosophy, considers a good philosopher to be also a good man. It is a truism to say that Socrates' philosophy is based on ethical considerations. A.E. Taylor, one of the renowned scholars of Greek philosophy, has the following to say about Socrates' approach to philosophy. "It was Socrates who, as far as can be seen, created the conception of the soul. . . . For more than two thousand years it has been the standing assumption of the civilized European man that he has *a soul*, something which is the seat of his normal working intelligence and moral character, and that, since this *soul* is either identical with himself or at any rate the most important thing about him, his supreme business in life is to make the most of it and do the best for it."[2] C.D. Broad[3] describes philosophy as 'critical thought', and stresses the analytic function of philosophy. On the other hand, Jose Ortegn Y Gasset proclaims the philosopher to be 'a specialist in universes'.[4] Philosophy for him is much more than science: the philosopher seeks integrated knowledge, vision of the wholeness of things. This, in my view, is the best description of the true nature of philosophy. This means that holism ought to be the proper endeavour of philosophy. It may be noted that holism is a philosophical theory, which holds that the whole has an existence of its own apart from the sum total of its parts.

Before discussing the emerging trends in philosophy in North-East India, it is imperative to discover various trends in philosophy in general. It is inappropriate to think that only sciences both natural and social have been changing, and that philosophy does not change at all. It is sometimes said that philosophy is a finished product: there is nothing new to be discovered or said in philosophy. But, this is not true as a matter of fact. Philosophy, historically speaking, began to find out the ultimate stuff of the world. The first philosopher of ancient Greece, that is, Thales, raised the question about the ultimate stuff of the world. Gradually, Anaxmandes, Anaximenes and many others followed the suit. The main concern of the ancient Greek philosopher was to find out through logical reasoning the ultimate stuff of the world. Various answers were given to the question, "what is the ultimate stuff of the world?" Water, air, fire, and sometimes four material elements were postulated as the basic stuff of the world.

With the appearance of Socrates, philosophy in Europe took a different turn. The shift was from Nature to Man. Socrates raised questions about justice, virtue, and many other related questions. In other words, ontological and ethical issues were the prime concerns of philosopher in Europe until the appearance of Kant on the scene. Kant gave a new turn to philosophy. He raised epistemological questions. For him, epistemological issues are questions relating to knowledge. Therefore, he is of the view that these questions relating to knowledge, especially human knowledge, must be answered first before we enquire on any enquiry.

The beginning of 20th century witnessed a new trend in philosophy. Instead of asking questions about nature, man and God, philosophers began to raise question about philosophy itself. In other words, philosophers became suspicious about ontology, metaphysics, epistemology, and so on. The so called basic questions relating to the basic stuff of the universe were ridiculed. This movement is known as Logical Positivism. Though it originated in Vienna in the European continent, yet it found its chief spokesman in A.J. Ayer in Great Britain. The age old questions were not only ridiculed by the logical positivists but metaphysics was derided as nonsense. Metaphysicians were characterised as patients and criminals, who had violated the logic of language. Therefore, they stand in need of treatment, the logical positivists aver.

With the appearance of Ludwig Wittgenstein on the philosophical scene, philosophy took yet another different turn. Piecemeal linguistical conceptual analysis became the watchword of philosophy. Great Britain became the home of this type of philosophy. The departments of philosophy at Oxford and Cambridge provided oven and hearth to new ideas to be cooked, transmitted, and supplied to different parts of the globe. G.E. Moore, Gilbert Ryle, J.L. Austin, and many others in Great Britain took great interest in what is variously called conceptual analysis, linguistic analysis, piece meal analysis, ordinary language analysis, and common sense philosophy. Philosophers like G.E. Moore and others began to defend common sense. The grand theories of metaphysics and ontology were rejected. Philosophers now turned their attention to analysis of ordinary language.

Great Britain and its ex-colonies in Asia, Africa, Australia and North-America became the centres of ordinary language philosophy. The credit goes to one single man, that is, Wittgenstein, a man from Austria of the European continent for changing the course of philosophy in the 20th century. But the continental Europe did not accept the so called conceptual analysis wholeheartedly. In some of the North-American and European universities, Philosophy of Science and Mathematical Logic began to replace Metaphysics including Phenomenology, Existentialism, and even ordinary language philosophy.

We must now draw our attention to the Indian scene. It is sometimes said (perhaps jocularly) that every Indian is a born philosopher. However, there is some truth in this joke. India is one of the countries in the world which produced various systems of philosophy, and philosophers with originality and insight. When the entire Europe including America were in the dark, India produced great works in philosophy, astronomy, astrology, prosody, poetics and grammar. But, due to various social and political reasons, Indian philosophy came to a halt. After the advent of the European on the Indian soil, Indian philosophy was revived. The Western orientalists like Wilkins, William Jones, Maxmuller, and many others showed keen interest in Sanskrit and consequently in Indian philosophical traditions. The discovery of Sanskrit by European Indologists played an important role in this respect. Indian scholars like Das Gupta, Hiriyana and Radhakrishnan wrote in English on Indian philosophical traditions. The attempts of the scholars like Maxmuller and others were to show the superiority of Indian thought over European counterparts. On the other hand, scholars like Radhakrishnan tried to discover the European counterparts in Indian philosophical traditions. There is a Hegel in Europe: there is a Ramanuja in India. There is a Bradley in Europe: There is a Shankar in India. This trend can be attributed to nationalist feelings not only in politics but also in academics. In the first part of the 20th century the philosophy departments of Indian universities were dominated by classical Indian philosophy and both classical and modern European philosophy. Plato, Aristotle, Descartes, Spinoza, Leibniz, Locke, Berkeley, Hume, Kant, Hegel, Fichte, Schelling and the six systems of Indian philosophy like Jainism, Buddhism, Nyaya-Vaisesika, Sankya-Yoga and Vedanta were the chief subject matter. Even Logical positivism could not enter the portals of Indian universities. It is only after some Indian scholars went abroad and studied there that modern European philosophies like Logical Positivism, Conceptual Analysis, Phenomenology and Existentialism made their entry into Indian universities. A.R. Wardia (Contemporary of Radhakrishnan and Hiriyana) was one of the first students who have gone abroad to study philosophy. Wardia spent more than a decade in studying philosophy in London, Cambridge and Oxford. He confuses in his writings that the so called new trends in European philosophy did not have any attraction for him. He writes, 'metaphysics is my home.' He came back to India, became Vice-Chancellor, and subsequently member of Rajya Saba. Though Radhakrishnan and T.R.V. Murthy were Spalding Professors in Oxford University and yet they did not have any attraction towards contemporary British philosophy. S.N. Das Gupta taught in Cambridge. He translated a large number of classics in Indian philosophy to English. But, he never took any interest in studying contemporary British philosophy, what to speak of European philosophy. Thus the philosophy departments of Indian universities were interested in mainly teaching classical metaphysics and epistemology both Indian and Western. G.L. Metha, one of the early Indian scholars, who went abroad and studied phenomenology and existentialism. After coming back to India, he introduced existentialism in his own university, that is, Benares Hindu University. This is how Existentialism gained some foothold in Indian universities. J.N. Mohanty is another scholar who had gone to Germany to study Phenomenology. After coming back to India, he introduced courses in Phenomenology in Burdwan, Vishva Bharati and Calcutta Universities.

G. Misra was a direct student of A.J. Ayer in London. After coming back to India, he introduced the teaching of Logical Positivism and contemporary British philosophy including conceptual analysis in Utkal University, where he worked. Rajendra Prasad was the first indian philosopher, who had studied analytical moral philosophy in Michigan University. And, after coming back to India, he introduced that subject in the University of Patna and Indian Institute of Technology, Kanpur, where he worked. This is how contemporary European philosophy made its entry into Indian universities.

After sixties, because of fresh cross fertilization of ideas of Europe and India, a new trend emerged, which was to assert one's own philosophy. An attempt was made by G. Misra, Daya Krishna, J.N. Mohanty and B.K. Motilal to discover and assert the philosophical contributions of India. Vendanta, Buddhism and Nyaya were taken as paradigms.

As matter stands today in India, the scope and domain of philosophy has extended and increased in Indian universities. It is not only that scholars are looking afresh at Indian philosophical traditions but also are contributing in their own ways to the analytical tradition of philosophy. In other words, the departments of philosophy in Indian universities are becoming open and flexible to new ideas from the West. However, the degree of openness varies from region to region. The southern universities particularly in Madras and Andhra Pradesh still do not look favourably to contemporary analytical philosophy.

Both Madras and Andhra Universities had the great fortune of having Radhakrishnan on their faculties. T.M.P. Mahadevan, a close student of Radhakrishnan, held the chair of Indian philosophy in Madras University for more than three decades. He was convinced that the so called analytical philosophy is just an aberration of thought. He was also convinced that Vedanta philosophy is the only philosophy. Madras university is the only university in India which gives two degrees in philosophy, that is, one in Indian philosophy and another in general philosophy.

Philosophy departments in North India of Bihar, Uttar Pradesh and Madhya Pradesh are still on the cross roads. They have not yet decided whether to lay emphasis on Indian philosophy or contemporary European philosophy. The eastern region, Orissa, Bengal including North-East are highly flexible and open. Before the creation of Gauhati University in 1948, students from the North-East were going to Calcutta University to study philosophy. Calcutta university too was not very open until recently in framing syllabi, which would include contemporary themes. The philosophy syllabi of Calcutta University began with Plato and ended with Fitche and Schelling with a heavy dose of Indian philosophy and psychology. Patna University was no exception. As far as we know, the first Khasi who had done M.A. in philosophy was R.R. Thomas.

The department of philosophy of Gauhati University started with a teacher, Patnaik, who had his M.A. degree from Calcutta University. It is no wonder therefore he framed syllabi in philosophy in Gauhati University on the model of Calcutta University. Das, who was the first professor of philosophy in Gauhati University did not introduce contemporary European philosophy at all. Instead, the faculty members were teaching the same old courses in philosophy, Kant, Hegel, Vendanta with a heavy dose of psychology. Kutty from Kerala, who studied at Banaras Hindu University, took over the reins of the department of philosophy from Das. His training at Benares did not allow him to introduce contemporary analytical philosophy in the department. Though some young scholars like A.P. Rao, B. Pahi, Gopal Khan and K.K. Bagchi joined the department, they left in due course of time for various reasons. The senior teachers of Gauhati University had degree either from Banaras, Calcutta, or Gauhati. The second university in the region is Dibrugarh University. For long many years it did not have post graduate department in philosophy. Only two years back it started post graduate programme in philosophy in one of its affiliated colleges, namely, Sibsagar College. The department is yet to take off research programme in philosophy. North-Eastern Hill University (hereafter referred to as NEHU) is the third university in North-East India, and the first central university, which came into existence in 1973. The department of philosophy was started in 1974. The reader and first head of the department had training in philosophy in Cambridge University under the able guidance of Bernard Williams, one of the greatest living and well known philosophers of modern times. Before the coming of NEHU, colleges were affiliated to Gauhati University, and therefore even in under graduate courses in philosophy, psychology occupied a major chunk. Gradually, the post graduate department of NEHU expanded in terms of the strength of faculty. The department organised workshops to frame syllabi. The philosophy syllabi of NEHU are modern and upto date, which lay equal emphasis on classical, medieval and modern philosophy both eastern and western including phenomenology and existentialism. In nutshell, the core courses of the department consist of hisotry of philosophy (both eastern and western), logic (both philosophical and symbolic), analytic philosophy, moral philosophy, philosophy of mind, philosophy of sciences (both natural and social), and analytic philosophy of religion. Further, the department has introduced teaching programmes in environmental ethics and philosophy of culture with a pronounced emphasis on tribal culture. Philosophy of mind has replaced psychology. In view of the fact that psychology is an independent discipline, we have thought it proper not to include it in post graduate programme in philosophy.

Manipur is the fourth university in North-East India. It grew out of a nucleus of Jawaharlal Nehru University Campus at Imphal. The first teacher in the department of philosophy was a product of Gauhati University. Other teachers of this department had training in Madras and in NEHU. It seems that this university is not keen in accommodating new trends and thought in philosophy syllabi. Arunachal University is the fifth university in this region. Unfortunately, this University is yet to introduce philosophy both at Undergraduate and Postgraduate levels. Assam University at Silchar and Tezpur University at Tezpur were simultaneously created. Tezpur does not have a department of philosophy whereas Assam University has one. It is heartening to state that Assam University used the philosophy syllabus of NEHU in the beginning. The first professor of philosophy of Assam University had training in existentialism and phenomenology. The other teachers of the department had training either in Gauhati University or North-Bengal University or Calcutta University or Visva Bharati. This department is not averse to introducing new ideas and themes from both Indian and Western philosophies. Their new syllabi bear ample testimony of this innovation and adventure. Tripura did not have a university of its own until recently. The colleges of Tripura were affliated to Calcutta University. The Nagaland University does not have a post graduate department in philosophy as yet. It is hoped that the department will be started very soon.

Before I give any comment on the emerging trends in philosophy in North-Eastern region, I must say that there is no absolute truth and absolute methodology in philosophy. Most of the time the old insights are discovered and rediscovered in philosophy from time to time. Further, there is not a single method or technique of philosophizing. However, from this it should not be concluded that in philosophy there are no methods and no insights. As a matter of fact, certain trends, techniques and methods get entrenched in academics and become fashions in academic circles. Historically speaking, empiricism, rationalism, idealism, materialism, dialectics, positivism, conceptual analysis, phenomenology, existentialism, and so on have emerged as trends in philosophy. As I have said earlier, no trend in philosophy is absolute. In other words, the so called trends in philosophy emerge, disappear and re-emerge from time to time.

The trends including intellectual climate of a department could be ascertained only by taking into account the teaching and research programmes of the concerned department. Gauhati University, the first in this region, concentrated on classical Indian and Western philosophies in its teaching and research programmes until recent times. But, at present, it is giving adequate emphasis on analytical philosophy and symbolic logic both in teaching and research programmes. This is evident from the syllabus of the post graduate department and the research work done by the research scholars as well as the faculty members. Further, the department is also researching into Vaisnavism of Shankar Dev and the religions of the local tribes. In other words, the department has picked up the tone of Anglo-American philosophy.

The teaching and research programme of the post graduate department of philosophy in NEHU is upto date in the sense that it has been laying equal emphasis on both classical and contemporary philosophies. This is evident from the teaching and research programme of the department. Research works have been published in the areas of history of philosophy (both Indian and Western), analytical philosophy, philosophy of language, philosophy of social sciences, philosophy of religion, moral philosophy, philosophical logic, existentialism and applied ethics. One of the important features of the research programme has been to study the local tribal religion. Both at M. Phil and Ph.D. levels scholars have written theses on tribal culture and religion. To the question, 'What is the emerging trend in philosophy department of NEHU?' Our answer is that it is in consonance with the international trend in philosophy. In other words, NEHU is not lagging behind European universities either in teaching or research programme. This is quite evident from the teaching and research programme of the department. But this is not to say that we are qualitatively on equal terms with European universities. This is upto others to judge. But, we can emphatically say that so far as the method and technique are concerned NEHU is not lagging behind in pursuing the latest techniques. It may not be out of place to mention here that we have been offering innovative courses like philosophy of culture including tribal culture and 'Issues in contemporary India Society', to name a few. Further, this department of philosophy for many years in the past gave one compulsory course in philosophy of social sciences to all the research scholars registered in the School of Social Sciences (the department of philosophy belonged to this school in the past). Unfortunately, the practice of giving a compulsory course at the school level itself was dropped. Besides achievements and pitfalls, in a word it can be said that department of philosophy in NEHU has some claim (however small it may be) which other universities of the other parts of the region cannot claim. However, this is not to cast any aspersion on the quality of the other departments of philosophy in the region. Assam, Manipur and Tripura universities have just started their programmes. Therefore, it is premature and inappropriate to give any comment on the trends of their departments, particularly in research area. But, there are encouraging signs and indications to hope that these departments of philosophy will blossom brightly in this respect, that too in the near future.

**REFERENCES**


1. Ducasse, C.J., 1941. *Philosophy as a Science*, New York: Oskar Press, p. vii.
2. Taylor, A.E., 1956. *Socrates*, New York: Doubleday Anchor Books, pp. 132-133.
3. Broad, C.D., 1923. "Critical Thought" from *Scientific Thought*, New York: Humanities Press.
4. Jose Ortega Y. Gasset, , 1960. "What is Philosophy?" Reprinted from "What is Philosophy?" by Jose Ortega Gasset, Translated from the Spanish by Wilfred Adams, W.W. Norton and Company.

# APPENDIX

I have tried to show in my paper that the emerging trends in philosophy in North-East India are reflected in the much pronounced emphasis on Philosophy of Religion with special reference to tribal religions of North-East India and Philosophy of Culture with special reference to tribal cultures. The appendix is self-explanatory since it details the research works done in the above mentioned areas of philosophy. Only the department of philosophy of North-Eastern Hill University, Shillong, finds a place here, since relevant information about the other departments of philosophy of other universities of North-East is not available in spite of the best efforts made by me.

The department of philosophy was given Departmental Research Support (D.R.S.) Programme by the University Grants Commission; of India. And this conducted two separate research projects, namely (i) Rationality, Justification and Tribal Thought, and (ii) Philosophy of Religion in the Indian Context. These two projects were completed successfully.

**Prof. M. Miri**

*Books*

1. *The Linguistic Situation in North-East India*, (Ed.), N.E. Indian Council of Social Science Research, Shillong, 1982.
2. *The Tribal Situation: Continuity and Change*, (Ed.), Indian Institute of Advanced Study, Shimla, 1996.

*Articles*

1. "Secularism, Science and Plurality of Religions", *Religion and Plurality of Religion*, (ed.), S.C. Dube and R. Basilov, Indian Council of Social Science Research, New Delhi, 1980.
2. "Understanding People and the Science of Man," *NEHU Journal of Social Sciences and Humanities*, 1984.

*Ph.D. Supervised*

1. "The Idea of a World View and Understanding People."

**Professor (Mrs.) S. Miri**

*Books*

1. *Religion and Society of North-East India*, (ed), Vikas Publishing House, 1980.
2. *An Introduction to the Study of Tribal Religions*, Concept Publishing Company 1983.
3. *The Khasi World View: A Conceptual Exploration*, CRRID, Chandigarh, 1988.

*Articles*

1. "Holism in Khasi Religion", *The Tribes of North East India*, (ed), S. Karotemprel, 1985.
2. "The World View of the Khasis", *The Trumpeter, Journal of Ecosophy*, Vol. 10, No. 4, 1993.
3. "Nature and the Tribeman", *The Book Review*, Vol. XXI, No. 4, April, 1997.

*M. Phil Supervised*

1. The Ao Naga Religion.
2. Understanding Tribal Culture With Particular Reference to Thadou Tribal Culture of North-East India.
3. Khasi-Pnar Concept of Nature.

*Ph.D. Supervised*

1. Religious Belief with Special Reference to North-East India.
2. Revivalism in Khasi Society.
3. The Religious Form of Life in Assam with Special Reference to Vaishnavism of Shankardeva.
4. The Concept of Virtue in the Khasi World View.
5. The Good and Godly Man in the Liagmei Naga Tradition.

**Prof. N. Malla**

*Articles*

1. Cross Religious Comparison, *Gandhi Marg*, March, 1987.
2. The Secular and the Religions in Gandhi's Philosophy, *Gandhi Marg*, 1987.
3. Causality, Meaning and Culture, *Indian Philosophical Quarterly*, Poona, Vol. XIX, No. 2, 1992.

**Prof. M.M. Agrawal**

*Book*

1. *Ethnicity, Culture and Nationalism in North-East India*, (ed.), Indus Publishing Company, New Delhi, 1996.

*Article*

1. A Teleological Conception of Culture, *Manascarya*, 1996.

**Dr. C.R. Agera**

*Book*

1. *Religious Critique of Culture*, Intellectual Publishers, New Delhi, 1991.

*Articles*

1. "Two Biblical Myths of Creation: An Exploration in Ecological Philosophy", *Journal of Indian Council of Philosophical Research*, XIII: 3, 1996.
2. "Religion, Culture and Nature: An Essay in Ecological Philosophy", *Society and Culture in North-East India*, Delhi, ISPCK, 1996.

**Dr. Jagat Pal**

*Article*

1. "Analysis of the Concept of Culture", *Ethnicity, Culture and Nationalism*, (ed.) M.M. Agrawal, Indus Publishing Co., New Delhi, 1996.

**Dr. S.C. Daniel**

*Articles*

1. "A Note on Philosophical Analysis of the Khasi Language and World View", *Khasi World View: A Conceptual Exploration*, Sujata Miri, CRRID, March, 1988.
2. "Khasi Religion and Christianity — A Comparative Study", *Assam Diocesan Journal*, 1990.
3. "Understanding Tribal Lore by Means of Intention Theory of Meaning", *Tribal Thought and Culture* (ed.) B.N. Saraswati, Concept Publishing Company, 1991.
4. "Was Gandhi a Christian?" *Gandhi Marg*, January–March, 1994.
5. "Christianity and Culture", *Society and Culture in North East India: A Christian Perspective*, CISRS, ISPCK, Delhi, 1996.

**Mr. Xavier Mao**

*Article*

1. "Status of Mao Women", *Status of Naga Women in Manipur*, Lucy Zehol, Regency Publications, New Delhi, 1998.

**Dr. E.R. Tongper**

*Article*

1. "The Christian Response to Inter-Cultural Dialogue in North-East India", *Society and Culture in North-East India: A*

*Christian Perspective* (ed.) S.K. Chatterji, CISRS, ISPCK, Delhi, 1996.

It must be noted that I have selected only books and articles of the above mentioned scholars which are relevant to the emerging trends in philosophy in North-East India. Needless to say that they have published many more books and articles in other areas.

# 7

# Trends in Sociological Research in North-East India (1947–97)

*Nikhlesh Kumar*

Our task was to pick up all the sociological works between 1947–1997. This time-frame, to our mind, had no particular academic justification. It rather had an emotional justification as this period marked the Golden Jubilee of the Indian Independence. Obviously, therefore, no academically essential relationship could be presumed between this period and the kind of issues presented in the relevant literature.

The term 'north-eastern region' has a politico-geographical connotation and designates a cluster of seven states along the north-eastern international border of India. Arunachal Pradesh, Assam, Manipur, Meghalaya, Mizoram, Nagaland and Tripura are the seven states in the region.

These seven states of the region are inhabited by a variety of societies occupying the plain and the hill areas. These societies, speaking different languages and practicing different forms of agriculture, show different structural and cultural characteristics. Historically speaking, these societies have undergone different experiences during the pre-British and the British periods. Whereas, the societies in the plains and the valleys have their histories in the documented form, the societies on the hills have preserved their experience in their folklore. An interesting observation is that whereas in the pre-British period these societies interacted with each other on their own terms either in the market-places or the battle-fields, the British introduced new terms of interaction through various politico-administrative and military measures. One important aspect of the British approach was to promulgate administrative orders restricting free interaction between the hills people and the plains people under the pretext that such an interaction would corrupt the people living on the hills.

Different north-eastern societies reacted to such measures differently in both the British and the post-British periods. However, during the post-British period, i.e., during the glorious half-a-century period of independent India these different societies put up their own terms of interaction as well not only with each other within the region but with others also in the Indian Union. These empirical realities provided a fertile field for investigation to the scholars belonging to various social science disciplines.

The British civil and military administrators had started documenting the descriptions of these societies for administrative convenience. Other accounts also started appearing in print in the form of travelogues and monographs prepared by Christian missionaries and others. All these accounts provided background information to the Indian scholars in the post-British period.

The first fifty years of Indian independence were marked by the growth in the institutions of higher learning in the region. The dependence on the university in Calcutta thus started weaning away. A university came up in Guwahati (Assam) in 1948 which subsequently started giving instructions in the discipline of Anthropology. Another university came up at Dibrugarh (Assam) in the mid-1960s and a department of Sociology was opened there. Even the Calcutta University started a department of sociology after it had come at Dibrugarh. The second department of Sociology in the region came up in 1976 at Shillong. This department was opened in the North-Eastern Hill University (NEHU) which had its post-graduate campuses at Nagaland and Mizoram. The campus at Nagaland was later on de-linked with NEHU and became the nucleus for a full-fledged university there. Assam University at Silchar (Assam) is also contributing to the teaching and research in the field of Sociology. Mention must be made here of the Department of Sociology at the University of Delhi which through its North-East Hill Area Programme has been training the youth from this region for more than three decades.

All these departments have also been engaged in carrying out researches on the various societies of the region. These researches are (i) self-proposed in the form of researches at the post-graduate and doctoral levels by the students, and those carried out by individual teachers; and (ii) sponsored by funding agencies in the form of research projects and invited research contributions in the seminars organised by various institutions. In addition to these the Anthropological Survey of India and the departments of Tribal Research in the various states of the region contribute to the research on the societies in their states. During the last two decades many research organizations have come up in the region in the non-governmental sector. These organizations help in the promotion of research activities by conducting research; organizing seminars; and publishing monographs, edited volumes, and project-reports.

The first fifty years of independence saw a proliferation of sociological literature as a result of various academic activities as explained above. The published and unpublished literature is available in the form of books, articles in research journals, mimeographed proceedings of various seminars and symposia, research project reports, dissertations submitted by research students for various research degrees. For the sake of convenience we decided to focus our attention on literature produced in the assigned period in the form of books only.

Before locating the literature produced during these fifty years we laid down two criteria for classifying any piece of literature as sociological. Firstly, a particular work should have used the conceptual framework of sociology in its explanation. Secondly, the work should have been based on the scientific methodology of sociology. In other words, we had to identify such works which were produced by those who were trained in thinking and writing sociologically.

Our analysis is based on 373 monographs and edited works in the English language. By scanning the bibliography we classified the titles state-wise. But there were some edited works which could not be put under any particular state because these contained articles either on the region as a whole or on several states. Such works were put, therefore, under another category labeled by us as 'General'.

We found that the maximum number of titles (24.66%) came under the category 'General', followed by the titles on Assam (20.11%), Arunachal Pradesh (14.75%), Meghalaya (14.48%), Manipur (7.77%), Nagaland (7.51%), Tripura (6.97%) and Mizoram (3.75%).

Works under the category 'General' were either a collection of articles written by different authors and edited by a single author; or these were a collection of papers presented in seminars by various invitees and edited by a single person or a group of persons. However, some of the works under the other categories were also either edited works or those produced by a team of authors.

An analysis of the dates of publication of the books brought out another interesting fact to light. There appears to be sudden spurt in the literature from the beginning of 1980. The decade of 1980 saw almost a three-fold increase in the publications as compared to the decade of 1970 and much more than those produced before 1970. It may not be wrong to infer even on the basis of an impressionistic and rough estimate that the number of books published in the decade of 1980 was much more than double of those published since the time of independence to the end of the decade of 1970. This spurt in the academic activities, however, is not unique to the period of 1980s only judging by the fact that the present incomplete decade of 1990s is also witnessing a sustained rate of publication of literature.

While scanning through the bibliography on the north-east we came across certain works related with some other social science disciplines, e.g., Political Science, History and Economics. We thought that some of these works were useful as reference and background material for sociological inquiry.

On the basis of our analysis we could identify the following issues in the literature surveyed by us:

### *Tribal Ethnography*

Studies have been conducted on the structural and cultural features of individual tribes inhabiting the hill areas of the north-eastern region. Some monographs were produced on the life in tribal villages. These villages being mono-tribal the books provide descriptive material on the tribal ethnography. A small number of works focused their attention only on the demographic features of the tribes.

Mention must be made here of the works produced by the scholars of the Tribal Research Institute of Arunachal Pradesh on the various tribes of the state.

### *Description of Institutions in Tribal Societies*

Studies have been conducted on the different institutions in the tribal societies. Monographs have been written on political, economic and religious institutions. Some studies discuss the socio-economic status of different societies while some others describe the occupational structures in some of the tribal societies.

### *Studies on the Customary Laws*

There are some studies on the customary laws of the tribal societies and the pattern of crimes in these societies. These studies have tried to codify the traditional laws in order to present a standardized version as against the regional variations in the societies. Since these customary laws show regional variations within the tribes the impact of such uniform codes should have been studied but we did not come across any reference on this point.

### *Studies on the Belief-System*

Some monographs were found on the systems of belief in tribal societies, their festivals, folktales, folklore and indigenous crafts and arts. These studies provide rich materials on these subjects. The literature has been produced more on the style of cultural anthropology. The social relational dimensions are found to be missing from these works.

### *Agricultural Practices and Land Tenure Systems*

A sizable contribution has been made by the studies on the agricultural practices and land tenure systems in the tribal societies. Such studies bring out the wide spectrum of agricultural practices from shifting cultivation to settled cultivation in different societies. Some studies throw light on the land laws and the land tenure systems. What we do not find in these studies are the aspects of the organisational frame of their economic activities and the division of labour in the society.

### *Change, Development, and the Impact of Various Government-sponsored Developmental Schemes*

These are the other areas in which a significant contribution has been made both on the tribal and the non-tribal societies. Most of the works in these areas are in the form of compilation of articles by various scholars. Attention has been focused on various developmental issues concerning the region, e.g., manpower development, agricultural development, industrial development, infrastructural development etc.

### *Studies on Ethnic Unrest and Protest Movements*

Issues of ethnic identity, conflict, protest movements by socio-political and students organizations have also been attended to by the academic community. Attempts have also been made in some of these studies to offer causal analyses of the states of tension and conflict at the intra- and inter- societal levels. Of course such causal analyses lack empirical bases.

### *Status of Women*

Recently some studies have come up in the area of the women's studies. The available studies have tried to describe the traditional status of women in the tribal societies.

The above classification shows that a wide ranging issues and areas have been studied during the fifty years of India's Independence. Our understanding of the trend shows that the majority of the works could be broadly reclassified as those concerned with (i) the structural and cultural aspects of the societies; and (ii) the problems faced by the societies due to both the developmental measures and lack of development of these societies.

In the end we would like to highlight the following:

(i) Much less attention has been paid to the study of the societies living in the plains as compared to those living on the hills. We have a near total absence of studies on the structure of the Bodos, the Assamese, the Bengali societies in Assam as well as those living in Tripura and Manipur. Studies have also been lacking on the many societies of Mizoram and Nagaland.

(ii) These studies lack a comparative perspective. Even the descriptive studies though lacking depth in the perspective do not have much heuristic value.

(iii) The research work has not focused on the intra-community and inter-community conflicts and the mechanisms of adjustment in the region. Thus neither the elements of competition for resources nor the mechanisms of boundary maintenance by different societies could come out clearly in the studies on the ethnic unrest and protest movements.

(iv) Lastly, most of these works lack a rigour in the application of sociological concepts and empirical methodology of the discipline. Moreover, the practice of quantifying the data was also found to be quite uncommon.

# 8

# Trends in Garo Language and Literature, 1947–1997

*M.S. Sangma*

Prior to 1940, Garo literature was marked by two distinctive features, namely, Christian and School Text books. When the American Baptist Missionaries arrived at Garo Hills in the later part of the 19th century and began to preach, they realised that unless the spoken word is accompanied by written word in their own language, their labours will not bear any fruit. This understanding made them translate the whole Bible into Garo language and took fifty years, 1874–1924 to complete with the help of a few educated Garos. They also published a number of booklets and tracts on various aspects of the Bible and Bible stories. Both the Missionaries and local Christians also translated and composed a large number of hymns.

The Missionaries also realised that in order to enable the people to read the books, schools must be opened and text books published. This led them to prepare the text books from Lower Primary to Middle English school level. Thus, till the 1940s, publication of different books of the Bible and other related literatures, such as, *Pilgrim's Progress*, *Mirror of the Heart*, Sunday school lessons and other booklets, tracts and school text books formed the main contents of Garo literature. Though from the beginning, Bengali script was used as the script of the Garo literature, it was switched over to Roman script by the last decade of the 19th century.

Early 1940s brought about a new spirit among a few educated Garos in the study and publications. A handful of Garo young men and women who joined Cotton College, Guwahati formed themselves into an Association and started a Garo periodical known as *"A'chik Ku'rang"* or the Voice of the Garos in 1940 under the guidance and editorship of Prof. Howard Denison Momin, who was then a lecturer of English in Cotton College, Guwahati. The article published in the periodicals aroused a sense of patriotism and pride among them in their own cultural heritage and began to look up to their own cultural roots. Thus with the first flash of enthusiasm and with renaissance spirit, the college and high school Garo students packed the periodicals with articles on poetry and prose on different aspects of Garo culture and oral traditions. A stage was thus set for study and development of secular Garo literature.

The development of secular literature during the last fifty years, 1947–1997 took place in various forms, such as, in the field of Poetry, Drams, Novel, Essays, Garo Proverbs and Phrases, Biography, translations from other literatures etc.

## Development in Garo Poetry

Till early nineteen forties, Garo poetry consisted mainly of hymns, translated and composed by both the Missionaries and the local literates. Some poems were of course, composed by the Garo literates specifically for the school text books which were rhythmical containing moral lessons. Of course, quite a few Garo L.P. school teachers composed a number of poems out of their own interests and left them unpublished which were discovered by their grand-children, many of which found their places in different issues of Garo journals and in the anthologies which are today prescribed for studies both in the under-graduate and post-graduate classes. But with the publication of "A'chik Ku'rang" (The Voice of the Garos) from 1940 onwards and other journals, hundreds of poems, mainly of local themes were published. The Garo poems can be broadly divided into two categories — (1) Collection and Compilation of Garo Sacrificial rites, Chantings and Charms, and (2) Modern Poetry both translated and composed.

(1) The Garo Sacrificial rites and Magical Charms consist of invocations to the respective deities during the religious ceremonies held at different stages of Jhum cultivation, sickness, marriage, death, excessive rain and drought and for protection and safeguard of the whole village and during any natural calamity.
(2) Modern Poetry (composed): This category of Garo Poems is based on various themes, such as, love, hatred, nature and natural beauties of Garo Hills on various seasons of the year, inheritance, poverty, patriotic poems etc.

Tagore's Gitanjali and Rubaiyat of Omar Khayyam were also translated besides other adapted poems, such as, Elegy written on a Country Churchyard, etc. Thus the last fifty years produced the greatest number of poems which are mostly secular in nature.

## Drama

In a pre-literate society, staging of drama was unknown to the Garos. But with the introduction of education and Christianity, the Christians began to enact tableau on Christmas eve. They also began to stage some drama based on the traditional Garo stories but the dialogues were not properly written and much depended on the ability of the persons to act and speak. But even those dramas staged, could no longer be traced.

The first work on Garo drama was published by Keneth Momin in 1969 entitled Nokdang or Family. This drama depicted the social and economic conditions of the Garos during the nineteen forties to sixties.

Out of 17 publications during the last fifty years, eight plays, namely, Nokdang (The Family), Kamni Bite (Fruit of one's action), Sin'kari (Winter), Janggil Kom'chik Nokma Sakgni, (Two hunched-back chiefs), Skul Master, Togan Sangma, Togan Matgrik and A'kim (clan bond) deal with modern contemporary social and economic conditions and idiosyncrasies of persons; two plays by Karnesh R. Marak, namely, Macbeth is an adaptation from the original 'Macbeth', Veniceni Badinggipa is a translation from "The Merchant of Venice" both by Shakespeare.

The seven remaining pays are based on the Garo legendary figures whose mighty deeds and heroic acts are still the subjects of stories told from father to son. The themes of the stories and the language in those plays are based on legendary stories which have become obscure to the present generation of the Garos and as such, they are considered to be difficult plays.

**The Garo Folklore**

The Garo folklore by S.R. Snagma and J.D. Marak contains 15 stories, whereas, Garo folklore by D.K. Sangma in three volumes contains 145 stories. These are simple stories similar to that of Aesop Fables, some of which, deal with the following —

1. The frog and the monkey
2. The elephant and an ant
3. Two sisters sleep in the Jhum field
4. The firefly and the monkey
5. The peacock's neck
6. The elephant and the porcupine
7. The woman, dimre
8. The jackal
9. The owl
10. The ghost
11. The crab
12. The monkey and the tortoise
13. The man called Chongchongminda
14. The dove
15. The man called Tengton, and so on

The folktales by D.S. Rongmuthu deal with the traditional stories on the creation of the world, water, man and all that there in. It also deals with the origin of fire and trees etc. A section of it also contains about the origin and migration of the Garos, their settlement in Garo Hills, origin of clans etc.

**Stories**

Besides the folklores and folktales, the Garos have also published books of stories, some of which have been based on the traditional stories. These stories centre round legendary heroes and heroines whose mighty deeds of valour are sources of admirations and inspirations. There are also stories which have bene created by the authors themselves within their cultural milieu. There are also stories translated or adapted from famous stories of other lands.

## Proverbs and Phrases

This branch of literature has come out in the form of publications only within the last two decades or so. Otherwise, they were all there in the mouths of the people, told and re-told on appropriate occasions.

## Essays and Compositions

The last three decades also witnessed a number of publications on essays and compositions or a collection of essays compiled from articles published in different Garo journals and periodicals. Some of these essays and compositions are meant for the school and college students to improve their writing skills, whereas, some of these publications are compilations of well-written essays and articles published in various Garo journals and periodicals which are today prescribed as text books for schools and colleges.

## Dictionary

Out of eight publications on dictionary, Ramke Momin's Bengali-Garo Dictionary contains about forty five thousand words and H.W. Marak's Garo-English-Assamese Dictionary has about 8–9 thousand words and Rangam Momin's English-Garo Dictionary contains about 6–7 thousand words. The others have about 4–5 thousand words but are authentic and very useful to the students.

## Novel

Out of five novels produced so far, I.R. Marak's Chigit-chakgreni Nokma and Gamseng are the product of her own imaginations and literary skill, whereas, Redin Monin's Khalsin and Sonatchi is based on the traditional love story of Khalsin and Sonatchi. Sonabal Me'chik by Simison Sangma is an adaptation, it is presumed, from Taranth Ganguli's Swarnalota and M. Rongmuthu's Mama Tomni Jamdap is a translation from Herriet Beecher Stowe's Uncle Tom's Cabin.

## Translated Works

Besides original works, a number of translated works have also been published during the last fifty years. Most of the translated works are famous books, such as, Pilgrim's Progress, Stories from Shakespeare, Arabian Nights, stories of Rabindranath Tagore, Ramayan, Helen of Troy etc. Though these are translated but they add to the literary standard of the Garo language.

## Garo Literary Criticism

This aspect of literature is still in its infant stage. Whatever books have been published on this line have been still elementary in their nature. The book on Rhetoric and Prosody has been translated from the English book.

## Grammar

The books on grammar have been written in the same way, English grammars have been written. There is still no book on Garo grammar dealing from Garo language point of view.

## History

Literature on the history of the Garos, their language and literature is still very few. Research-based standard work on Garo history is still absent. Jobang Marak's Garo History and Moniram Marak's A'chikni Ma'biding deal with the origin and migration of the Garos from father to son. Levisond Sangma's history of the Garos and P.C. Kar's A'chik aro A'chik A'song are based mainly on the accounts given by Mackenzie in his History of Relations of British with the North-Eastern Frontiers of India.

Regarding the history of Garo literature, M.S. Sangma has exhaustively dealt in his History of Garo Literature, though it is in English and in a sketchy way in P.C. Kar's A'chik aro A'chik A'song.

M.S. Sangma's History of Garo Language is the only book dealing with the origin and development of Garo language so far. It traces the probable origin of the language and subsequent borrowings of different Indian and English languages.

## Biography

The biographies published on local personalities depict also the socio-political and economic conditions of the people of that time besides new informations on the persons concerned, the biographies on other eminent personalities helped the people to gauge the greatness of people of other lands.

## Religion

The list of published works on religion is not exhaustive but it contains the main trend in the development of religious literature in Garo language.

Out of the list, the book by L.R. Marak entitled 'Bebera'ani Bimik' deals with the basis of Garo animistic religious beliefs. It deals with the origin of Garo deities and various deities with their powers and functions and describes how they control the action of man and the duties of man towards them. It also deals with encantatious and contains creation stories of the world, man and other animate and inanimate objects.

Other works deal with different aspects of Christian religion, such as, Pastor's handbook, how to run the best sunday schools, God and Man and their relation, Love your neighbour, Christ will come back, Bible commentary, Life of Christ, Christian Leadership, Purgatory, Songs of Solomon, etc. There are also in the list that deal with the biographies of the famous Queens in the Bible, Ruth and Joan of Arc.

Though the publications on religion deal essentially with Christian and Garo religion, some of these publications have literary value and thus enhance the literary standard of Garo literature.

In conclusion, it can be said that the last fifty years, that is, from 1947–1997 produced the greatest number of secular literatures in Garo language than ever before. From confining themselves to that of Christian literature and school text books alone, it crossed over to the production of various kinds of secular literatures. But of all the branches of Garo secular literature, it was in the field of poetry that the Garos have made the greatest advance.

## SELECT BIBLIOGRAPHY (1947–1997)

*Anthologies*

1. D.S. Rongmuthu, Apako Gisik Ra'anio, Calcutta, 1949. (In Memory of My Father)
2. D.S. Nengminza, Seokgimin Poetryrang, Calcutta, 1958. (Selected Poems)
3. H.W. Marak, A'chik Aganbewalrang, Gauhati, 1959. (Original Tales of the Garos)
4. H.W. Marak, Rubaiyat of Omarkhayyam (Tr.), Gauhati, 1960.
5. E.R. Marak, Chimonggimin A'chik Ku'rang, Tura, 1961. (Collected Garo Poems)
6. B.S. Bangshall, Sonajing Bak I, Tura, 1962.
7. B.S. Bangshall, Sonajing Bak II, Tura, 1964.
8. H.W. Marak, Gitanjali (Tr), Tura, 1966.
9. Rev. Tilokchand Momin, Songkristan, Tura, 1968.
10. K.M. Momin, Chasong Gital A'chik Poetry, Tura, 1973.
11. Rev. Gilbert Marak, Ang Gisik Ku'aning, Tura 1973.
12. L.D. Shira, A'chik Poedorang, Bidol I, Calcutta, 1983.
13. Art & Culture, Govt. of Meghalaya, Ripinggimin Poedorang, Shillong, 1991.
14. E.Ch. Marak, Biporinni Katta, Tura, 1996.
15. L.D. Shira, A'chik Poedorang, (Garo Poems), Bidol II, Tura, 1997.

*Drama*

1. K.M. Momin, Nokdang (The Family), Tura, 1969.
2. A.G. Momin, Kamni Bite (Fruit of One's Action), Tura, 1969.
3. Karnesh R. Marak, Macbeth (Adaptation), Tura, 1970.
4. Cartin R. Marak, Sinkari (Winter), Tura, 1981.
5. J.R.L. Marak, Janggil Kom' chik Nokma Sakgni, Shillong, 1983.
6. L.R. Marak, Dikki, Bak I, Tura, 1983.
7. L.R. Marak, Dikki, Bak II, Dhubri, 1984.

8. Karnesh R. Marak, Muga Dingsepa, Tura, 1984.
9. J.R.L. Marak, Aje aro Gilje, Shillong, 1984.
10. L.D. Shira, Skul Master, Dhubri, 1985.
11. L.R. Marak, Metongbolni Gittim, Tura, 1987.
12. L.R. Marak, Pa Togan N. Snagma, Tura, 1987.
13. J.R.L. Marak, Serejing aro Waljan, Shillong, 1988.
14. L.R. Marak, Dikkini Gro Dinga, Tura, 1989.
15. H.N. Sangma, Togan Matgrik, Tura, 1991.
16. Karnesh R. Marak, Veniceni Badinggipa (Tr), Shillong, 1995.
17. Barthon G. Momin, A'kim, Tura, 1995.

*Folklore*

1. S.R. Sangma and J.D. Marak, A'chik Golpo, Tura, 1927 Ist ed. 1957 Re-print.
2. D.K. Sangma, A'chik Golporang, Part I, II, & III, Tura, 1963 1st ed.
3. D.S. Rongmuthu, Apasong Agana (As My Father Tells), Tura, 1970, 1st ed.

*Stories*

1. Suddhindra Marak, Sylsehni Katta Rongchu, Goalpara, 1951, 1st ed.
2. Bimolin Momin, Mingsinggipa Golporang, Tura, 1957.
3. N.B. Sangma, Kandikgipa Golporang, Tura, 1964.
4. J.R.L. Marak, Niba Jonja-Aje Gilje, Shillong, 1989, 1st ed.
5. J.R.L. Marak, Gonga Raksanpa, Gongsa Terapa, Shillong, 1991.
6. J.R.L. Marak, Dambo aro Rongjengni Nongchram, Shillong, 1991.
7. S.J. Sangma, Ambini Golpo, Shillong, 1993.
8. K.M. Momin, Duk Man'gipa Kalang aro Gipin Golporang, Dhubri, 1997.

*Garo Proverbs (Wise-Sayings) and Phrases*

1. M.S. Sangma and J.R.L. Marak, Agan Me'apa (Proverbs), Shillong, 1985.
2. B.K. Sangma, A'chik Katta Ku jikse (Phrases), Tura, 1990.
3. B.G. Momin, Chimonggimin A'chikrangni Bebe Ra'anirang, Tura, 1991.
4. J.R.L. Marak and M.S. Sangma, Ku'jikse, Shillong, 1991.
5. W.K. Sangma, A'chik Kattarang, Tura, 1991.
6. B.K. Sangma, Agan Me'apako Dilbadale Seani, Tura, 1996.

*Essays and Compositions*

1. K.M. Momin, A'cik Composition, Goalpara, 1970.
2. K.M. Momin, A'chikni Chanchibewale Seanirang, Dhubri, 1972.
3. J.B. Sangma, Chisakni Katta, Tura, 1975.
4. Donald N. Sangma, Nambate Janggi Tanganina Skie Ra'anirang, Shillong, 1978.
5. Mihir N. Sangma, Maniani Bidik, Calcutta, 1982.
6. Mihir N. Sangma, Pagitchamni Ku'bisring, Calcutta, 1982.

7. L.D. Shira, Kadimgimin Seanirang, Bak I, Calcutta, 1984.
8. L.D. Shira, kadimgimin Seanirang Bak II, Calcutta, 1984.
9. A.C. Momin, A'chikni Ku'andik, Tura, 1985.
10. Gilbert Marak, Gimaangengane Ama A'chik A'songde, Tura, 1993.

*Dictionary*

1. Ramke W. Momin, Bengali-Garo, Calcutta, 1887 (Bengali Script), Shillong, 1996, (Re-Print in Roman Script).
2. M.C.Mason, English-Garo, Calcutta, 1920.
3. Dingmin S. Nengminza, Garo-English, Calcutta, 1940, 1st Ed.
4. Dingmin S. Nengminza, English-Garo, Calcutta, 1954, 1st Ed.
5. Kandura W. Momin, English-A'chikku, Calcutta, 1955 1st Ed.
6. Rangam G. Momin, English-Garo, Calcutta, 1957, 1st ed.
7. H.W. Marak, Garo-English-Assamese, Gauhati, 1975.
8. A Group of Garos, Oxford Picture Dictionary, Calcutta, 1978.

*Novel*

1. Simison R. Sangma, Sonabal Me'chik, Allahabad, 1968, 1st ed.
2. Redin Momin, Khalsin aro Sonatchi, Calcutta, 1972, 1st ed.
3. M. Rongmuthu, Mama Tomni Jamdap, Dhubri, 1981. (Tr. Uncle Tom's Cabin).
4. I.R. Marak, Chigitchakgreni Nokma, New Delhi, 1984. (The Chief of Chigitchakgre)
5. I.R. Marak, Gamseng, Tura, 1994.

*Translated Works*

1. Wilson K. Marak, Songregipani Songreani, Madras, 1936 (Pilgrim's Progress) 1st ed. (many reprints).
2. Bimolin Momin, Mingsinggipa Golporang, Calcutta, 1957.
3. Wilson K. Marak, Rabindranath Tagoreni Basegimin Golporang, Shillong, 1962, 1st ed.
4. Mackenson Rongmuthu, Sin'karini Katta, (Winter's Tales), Tura, 1963.
5. Mackenson Rongmuthu, Veniceni Badinggipa, (Merchant of Venice), Tura, 1964.
6. N.B. Sangma, Sinbadni Skanggipa Songreani, Tura, 1965.
7. Wilson K. Marak, Rome Songjinmako Kama, Calcutta, 1966.
8. James Wood (Pub), Ka'donge Baltigipa, Gauhati, 1966.
9. Wilson K. Marak, Arabian Walrang (Arabian Nights), Calcutta, 1970.
10. Wilson K. Marak, Shakespeareni Golporang, Allahabad, 1971. (Stories from Shakespeare by Charles Lamb)
11. K.M. Momin, Ka'donggipa Matgrik (Benhur), Tura, 1975.
12. Redin Momin, Ramayan (Ramni Golpo), Tura, 1991.

*Garo Literary Criticism*

1. M.S. Sangma, Elements of Literary Criticism, Shillong, 1984 1st ed.
2. D.D. Shira, Gisik Matgrikrang, Tura, 1991.
3. V.B. Sangma, Rhetoric and Prosody (Tr), Tura, 1994.
4. L.D. Shira, Garo Literary Criticism, Tura, 1996.

*Grammar*

1. E.G. Phillips, Outline of Grammar of Garo Language, Shillong, 1904, 1st ed. Tura, 1988 Reprint.
2. Rangam G. Momin, English Grammar and Composition, Calcutta, 1939 1st ed. (Many reprints)
3. D.S. Nengminza, English Grammar and Translation, Calcutta, 1957, 1st ed.
4. Samson K. Sangma, A'chik Grammar, Calcutta, 1970.
5. Peter Rema, Mandi Grammar, Shillong, 1980.
6. Clearson K. Sangma, Primary Skul Garo Grammar aro Translation, Gauhati, 1983.

*History in Garo*

1. Jobang D. Marak, Garo History, Tura, 1930, 1st ed (Reprints).
2. K.W. Momin, History of Assam, Calcutta, 1952, 1st. ed.
3. K.W. Momin, History of India, Calcutta, 1953, 1st ed.
4. G.D. Marak, Origin and Beginning of Education and Civilization, Tura, 1955.
5. G.D. Marak, Ancient Man and Ancient World, Tura, 1955.
6. Levisond N. Sangma, History of the Garos, Tura, 1965.
7. P.C. Kar, A'chik aro A'chik A'song, Tura, 1973.
8. J.R. Marak, Jallianwalla Baghni Kattarang, Tura, 1978.
9. M.S. Sangma, History of Garo Literature, Shillong, 1983, 1st. ed.
10. M.S. Sangma, History of Garo Language, Shillong, 1995.
11. G.A. Marak, Meghalaya Stateko Maikai Man'aha, Tura, 1994.
12. Mihir N. Sangma, Gamagimin A'chikrangni A'dokrang, New Delhi, 1995.
13. Moniram R. Marak, A'chikni Ma'biding, Tura, 1997.

*Biography*

1. K.W. Momin, Ramke Miminni Janggi Tangani, Tura, 1957.
2. Wilson K. Marak, Sadhu Sundar Singh, Calcutta, 1967.
3. K.D. Sangma, Eisenhowerni Janggi Tangani, Tura, 1976.
4. K.D. Sangma, John F. Kennedyni Janggi Tangani, Tura, 1977.
5. Surendra S. Marak, Bong Laskerni Janggi Tangani, Shillong, 1980.
6. Surendra S. Marak, Gongsin S. Marakni Janggi Tangani, Shillong, 1982.
7. Surendra S. Marak, Jaran R. Sangmani Janggi tangani, Shillong, 1982.
8. K.R. Marak (Pub.), Autobiography of Ramke, Shillong, 1990.
9. Mihir N. Sangma, Capt. Williamson A. Sangma, New Delhi, 1992.

*Books on Religion*

1. Suddhindra Marak, Kristona Sigipa Pagitcham Manderang aro Constantine Raja, Jorhat, 1952.
2. Fr. F. Pianazzi, Pastor's Handbook, Tura, 1955.
3. N.A. Kirkwood, Gisik Rongtalgipako Uiani, Dhubri, 1964.
4. Hazel Morris, Nambatgipa Sunday Schoolrang, Gauhati, 1966.
5. James Wood (Pub), Isol aro Mande, Gauhati, 1966.
6. James Wood (Pub), Nang'ni Songsulna Ka'sabo, Gauhati, 1966.
7. Wilson K. Marak, Kristo Re'bapilgen, Gauhati, 1966.
8. Dr. P.S. Momin, Matini Gimin Seani, Gauhati, 1969.
9. Rev. Gilbert Marak, Sastroni Mingsinggipa Ranirang, Tura, 1974.
10. Rev. Gilbert Marak, Ruth, Tura, 1975.
11. Fr. Roger Dal Zovo, Jingwanni Chong'motgipa Mondoliko Ame Man'ani.
12. Fr. Mankin & Paul, Janggini Rama, Shillong, 1980.
13. Fr. Mankin, Jisu Kristoni Janggi Tangani, Shillong, 1981.
14. L.R. Marak, Bebera'ani Bimik, Tura, 1986.
15. Fr. A. Buccieri, Kristoko Daksningani, Shillong, 1987. (Tr. Immitation of Christ)
16. Fr. A. Buccieri, Kristian Bebera'ani, Shillong, 1989.
17. Fr. A. Buccieri, Ong'chenggipa Mondoli, Shillong, 1990.
18. Fr. A. Buccieri, O Gitel, Chingko Bi'na Skibo, Shillong, 1991.
19. Fr. A. Buccieri, Sasstrooniko Ambo, Shillong, Tura, 1992.
20. L.D. Shira, Kristianrang aro Jihudirangni Manianirang, Tura, 1992.
21. Fr. T. Mankin, Dilgipa Ong'ani, Shillong, 1992.
22. Shallindro Marak, Ra'angbo Gitelona, Tura, 1992.
23. Shallindro Marak, Chongipa Bilcham, Tura, 1993.
24. Fr. T. Mankin, Janggi Chiripram, Shillong, 1993.
25. Fr. T. Mankin, Katholik Mondolini Skotong, Shillong, 1993.
26. Fr. A. Buccieri, Watatarangni Kamrang, Tura, 1996.
27. Fr. A. Buccieri, Arc-ni Rongtalgipa Joan, Gauhati, 1996.
28. Fr. A. Buccieri, Solomonni Ring'ani, Tura, 1996.
29. Fr. A. Buccieri, Rt. Paulni Romanrangna Chiti, Tura, 1997.
30. Fr. A. Buccieri, Rt. Paulni Korinthrangna Chitirang, Tura, 1997.
31. K.M. Momin, Bilakbatsranggipa Matgrik, Dhubri, 1997.
32. Shallindro Marak, Mingsinggipa Kristianrang Maikai Kristoko Ma'sinchengaha, Tura, 1997.

# 9

# Trends in Assamese Literature: 1947–97

*B.K. Dev Sarma*

## Prelude

Without going into details of rich heritage of Assamese literature enhanced by pre-Vaishnav and neo-Vaishnav leaders, chiefly during Sreemanta Sankardev and his times, we can aptly remark that the base of modern Assamese literature has been made stronger by these literature. With the profusion and variety of the literature of such earlier periods, the ancient Assamese literature attained a full-grown stage. The royal support in this direction was one of the important factor. An example to support it: 'King Naranarayan (1540–1550) of Coach Behar while ordering Ram Saraswati to translate Mahabharata into Assamese sent to the poet's house several bullock-carts laden with manuscripts and supplied him with a contingent of servants and maids so that the poet might be free from worldly anxieties and devote himself, entirely to the work of translating the epic.'

But the British domination obtained through the treaty of Iyandabu ushered a set back in Assamese literature. The situation with regard to modern Assamese literature was summarised by S.K. Bhuyan in his article '*The Assamese*' published in "The Assam Review" of April, 1928 as ". . .For several decades after the British occupation of the country, Bengali was the language of the schools and the courts; and the influence of Bengali literature thus introduced has not been eradicated from the land. The Assamese author publishes a book at a loss, and he is naturally shy in repeating his financially unprofitable experiment by publishing another book. The Assamese are not whirled by the remote traces of any world movement, and hence no Assamese literature of the present day has occupied a position in the world-wide republic of human letters."

But inspite of all difficulties the total volume of Assamese literary production upto the end of second world war is not a negligible quantity. A host of writers studying in Calcutta and residing erstwhere outside Assam took to their literature seriously and caused the growth of modern romantic period in the history of Assamese literature. These literary champions and protogenists produced good dramas, poetries, social and historical novels, short stories depicting all phases of Assamese life and sufficient quantity of biographical literature. Even some books, though quantitatively smaller in number, on scientific subjects were produced under the auspices of the Assam Sahitya Sabha.

In fact, the growth of many reviews and periodicals, like Arunoday, Assam Bandhu, Jonaki, Bijuli, Usha, Banhi, Milan, Assam Sahitya Sabha Patrika, Awahan etc; enhanced the progress of modern Assamese literature to a great extent. The stalwarts of this period are Ananda Ram Dhekial Phukan, Gunabhiram Barua, Ratneswar Mahanta, Hemchandra Goswami, Kamala Kanta Bhattacharyya, Chandra Kumar Agarwala, Padma Nath Gohain Barua, Rajani Kanta Bardoloi and Lakshmi Nath Bezbarua. The growth of newspaper literature to spread knowledge of literature to the common people is another noteworthy factor of pre-independence period.

## Impact of 2nd World War Etc.

The pre-independence period, specially the fifth decade is a period of unrestness in social life of the Assamese due to August movement, second world war events, Gandhian movement, and communal riots destroyed the literary atmosphere. The critical economic condition was also a factor to deter literary growth in Assam. But on the other hand, the scientific as well as technological growth brought in during the 2nd World War period has affected the Assamese social life also and its reflection happens to be in the literary works. The independence of India has brought changes in the world of education of Assam by way of establishment of Gauhati University (1948) and also by the establishment of All India Radio at Shillong and Guwahati. Such happenings brought a new light towards the Assamese literature which attained a sort of static stage. The romantic trend set by Awashan and Banlu is replaced by progressive outlook, realism in social outlook and thus a new trend creeps in the Assamese literature. The birth of modern poems, socialistic novels and short stories push back the romanticism and usher in realism, in Assamese literature, although a great-cut interface is difficult to trace.

Yet, the difference between pre-war period and post war period after independence can be felt on ideals, material outlook and techniques in Assamese literature. The changing values towards life after independence have influenced the Assamese literature a lot. This new class of writers practically shows a revolutionary trend as compared to mechanical romanticism and social bonds. Instead, the new class of literature has given more stress on individual freedom, generation gap, social outbursts against unfounded beliefs, customs and blind religious faith and economic liberalism in order to bring new light of progress in the society. During pre-independence period the romantic supporters gave more stress on aristocratic class of people, self-centred attitude of the upper class and as a whole of the society. Whereas, the post-independence trend is on the critical analysis of the so-called aristocratic group, self-realisation and individualism. Psycho-analysis of Freud has been influencing this new group of writers. The influence of Marxism is another new trend prevailing in post-independence period.

In order to understand the new trend of Assamese literature after 1950, we are to consider each branch separately as (i) Poetry, (ii) Novel, (iii) Short Story, (iv) Essays, Travelogue etc., (v) Drama, (vi) Bio-graphy, (vii) Children Literature and (viii) Scientific Literature.

(i) *Poetry*: Let us first consider poetry where marked changes are seen. The romantic trend coupled with mysticism, spiritualism and patriotism continued upto sixties through the writings of Nilmani Phukan (elder), Ambikagiri Roy Choudhury, Pransanna Lal Choudhury, Naleeni Bala Devi, Ananda Chandra Barua. The new trend of modern poetry of symbolism though began with the fifth decade comes to lime light after sixties. Changes in the content, wordings, techniques, metre, imagery and even outlook have surfaced through the poets of sixties and after markedly.

Two basic trends can be seen through modern Assamese poetry. The older group believes in socialism though they do not deny the individual freedom. These Poets (like Hem Barua, Navakanta Barua, Nilmani Phukan (younger), Bhaben Barua, Ajit Barua, Hari Barkakati, Nirmal Prabha Bordoloi, Bireswar Barua, Mahendra Bora, Hiren Dutta, Homen Borgohain, Mahim Bora, and a few others) believe in the demand of time but like to maintain self-independence and own entity. They believe that human mind is so complex and wonderful that a particular socio-politico or economic ideology cannot solve the entire gamete of social problems. They also believe in keeping the doors and windows of the mind open; but equally they have faith in maintaining the tradition, rich cultural heritage and touch of romanticism.

On the other hand, the other group having followed the Marxist philosophy (like Hiren Gohain, Hiren Bhattacharyya, Amalendu Guha, Keshab Mohanta, Rabindra Sarkar, Hemanga Biswas, Bejon Lal Choudhury and a few others) has set the trend of poetry establishing naked reality that reflects social problems of day-to-day life due to modern civilization and culture.

It is observed that the new trend in Assamese modern poetry has been influenced by the western-wave of late nineteenth and early twentieth century's symbolic trend. The Japanese 'Hikoo' trend has also influenced the new trend in Assamese modern poetry. The mental horizon of the modern poets is extensive. They have enveloped the global elements coming out of old trend of mysticism, spiritualism and naturalism.

(ii) *Novel & Short Story*: I have already mentioned that the post-independent period of Assamese life is the outcome of the influences of the 2nd World War and the Independent Movement. That is why, the long lasting changes brought in by these two events are reflected through novels written after independence. The most of the novels written during the post-independence period are socialistic in nature coupled with the new world of reality. The influence of progressive outlook due to the progress of science and technology is also present in the writers of Assamese novels after 1950 onwards. In fact, these new writers have reflected through their novels a look at life in its bare reality.

After independence, specially from the late fifth decades, the Assamese society has undergone a few radical outbursts. The influx of foreign nationals, the problem of unemployment, the sense of negligence by the central government and the rise of socio-political sense among the youth groups are few of them. Such real problems have been influencing the novelists of Assamese literature specially after 1960.

Equally with such local changes, the global change under the influence of Freudian Psychology with a Marxist undercurrent has been reflected in the Assamese novel. In such writings, the faith for regeneration capacity of humanity is potent. The psychological environment of hopelessness is seen to influence the outlook of the present novelists of Assamese literature. Traditional as well as humanistic social values have lost validity in their writings. The process of disenhancement has been hastened by the grave position of pressing economic distress, social degeneration creating generation gap and youth's unrest. As a consequence of such new outlook, realism became a dominant tendency in Assamese modern literature as a whole, but especially in the realm of the novel and the short-story. The old trend of descriptive romanticism of historical events are replaced by day-to-day life situations and experiences in the new trend of Assamese novels and short stories.

(iii) *Drama*: The progress achieved in the post-independence prose and poetry of Assamese literature has not been achieved in drama sector. May be due to the poor condition of the theatrical halls and the influence of cinema the theatr could not compete and as a result the drama-writing suffere a set back during early post-independent period. But from th late sixties, the advent of moving theatrical group has inspire the dramatist to go ahead with new technique like play bac songs, flash-back lighting arrangements etc. and these tech niques have influenced the content and mode of Assames drama. The realism introduced by Ibsen, Becket etc. ha influenced the Assamese dramatists. Even the absurd drama street-drama and open-air drama are written in this period.

(iv) *Others*: Among others we can envelope biographies travelogue, essays, criticism including textual criticism, chil dren-literature and science-literature. In every phase, there ha been an upsurge of new trend which are comparable with th trends in the other parts of the country. This is rather a achievement of Assamese literature after independence. Hos of writers in these spheres well-versed with the global change have emerged out to produce master-pieces in their ow spheres. Quite a few left-critics have contributed much to wards the growth of this new trend. Science literature whic is rather inducted from the decade of sixty as a continuou effort though basically through science columns in dailies monthlies and weeklies. Science fiction is definitely a ne chapter added to the Assamese literary works after indepen dence, which is, periodwise, counted as modern period.

# 10

# Poetry and the English Writing Scene

*Ananya Sankar Guha*

In India the aesthetics of writing poetry in English was generally speaking looked down upon and, considered a second rate creative activity. However there arose in the '60s and '70s a cluster of powerful poets who reflected through their poetry a growing and foreboding sense of what popularly came to be known as 'Indianness'. They were also conscious of their own poetic idioms, styles and techniques. They were vigorous in experimenting and enhanced their poetry with a poetic vocabulary of their own. Their poetry was uninhabited, bespeaking of a brutal candour and marked by the kind of creative tension that generates good poetry. In the '80s and '90s emerged a group of well educated younger generation of poets, conscious of their craft, displacing a poetic meticulousness and resilience of poetic themes. They had a down to earth flexible approach varying their themes from love to social exposure and inquisition. Consequently the number of poetry journals grew among the literati of the country. There was also an interaction and interplay of ideas between the older generation of the Indian poets writing in English and the younger generation.

North East India too witnessed the emergence of such a younger group of poets in the 80s and early 90s whose poetry written in feverish moments of societal crisis attracted the attention of critics and literary journals of India and abroad.

Coincidentally these poets all live in Shillong and it was the poetry page of The Telegraph Colour Magazine edited by the celebrated Indo English poet Jayanta Mahapatra which gave them the opportunity to be published and break new grounds in the Indo English poetry scene. In the mid and late 90s the North East Forum For English Studies established in Guwahati, and formed mainly by some college teachers; and the North East Writers Forum consisting of creative writers in this part of the country devoted much of their energy in encouraging the art of poetry in English, in the region. This is being done through their journals *North East Forum For English Studies* and *Frontiers* respectively which devote a section to poetry written in English. These are in addition to *Lyric,* a journal devoted exclusively to poetry and founded by the Shillong poets mentioned above, in the late eighties.

The essay under discussion will focus on these poets from Shillong as certain binding themes of personal, social and historical concern unified their poetry and gave it a distinct flavour, typified as it was with an astonishing sense of lyricism. Music and its ineffable utterances are surely the soulmates of these poets and the very stuff of their poetry.

The poets who readily come to the mind are: Desmond Leslie Kharmawphlang, Robin. S. Ngangom, Kynpham SIngh Nongkynrih and Almond Dean Syiem protagonists and votaries of the poetry of feeling. Their verse immediately attracted critical attention for its universal concerns kneading these with localised themes. Their poetry was lyrical and original imbued with a striking poise, clarity and spontaneity. They empathized with one another in their themes, their 'influences' were many: Neruda, Arghezi, Gullen, Pessoa, Jayanta Mahapatra to name a few. Yet these 'influences' on their poetry did not limit or stultify their verse, rather they empathetically related experiences of these poets to their own poetic credos cleverly, deftly and passionately. They thrived on such a poetic fare for their personal reading, poetic sustenance; creating in the process an aura of their own, and a 'poetic wave' or movement in Shillong and North East India. All aspiring poets looked upon them approvingly as their mentors their 'gurus' as it were and the foundations of the Shillong Poetry Society were finally established. They believed in encouraging younger poets and helped them to publish their poetry in their mouthpiece *Lyric*. *Lyric* the poetry journal of the Shillong Poetry Society subsequently gained reputation as a standard poetry journal acclaimed by critics in Sahitya Akademi's *Indian Literature*, "The Times of India", "The Indian Express", "Business Standard" etc. *Lyric* published the works of poets on a national and international scale, and was scrupulous in its editing and selection. The chief architects of *Lyric* were the poets mentioned above though much of the pioneering work in publishing it was achieved by Robin Ngangom and Desmond Kharmawphlang.

Their poetry gave a continuity and compatibility to the Indian poetry writing scene though they spoke in a different voice from the poets of 'mainstream' India and expressed different points of view. Very soon they were attending poets' meet in different parts of the country organised by literacy and cultural bodies such as the Sahitya Akademi and Bharat Bhavan.

If we speak of a general 'Indianness' in poetry written in English in India these poets nonchalantly subverted such a notion by writing poignantly and memorably of their hometown, a shared nostalgia for the past, and the prevalent social issues with their attendant pitfalls. They evinced a remarkable racial, sociological and historical memory to capture iridiscent moments of their society in transition. Makarand Paranjpe the critic has described them as 'ethnic" poets. Yet this term is not to be construed negatively but as a means to their greater poetic ends. They are simple, yet astonishingly lyrical, complex yet not intellectually, they shun any sort of intellectualism in poetry and believe that the best of poetry and its finer instincts has the indelible stamp of the native genius, innate but untutored wisdom; and in William Wordsworth's decree is 'man speaking to man'. They glimpsed such a primal functioning in the best of poetry and attempted to encapsulate this in their verse. They used effectively the oral tradition and mythology of their cultures and related these appositely to their poetic vision, philosophy and craft. Above all they viewed the strenuous craft of writing poetry as essentially meditative and philosophical devoid of any hackneyed 'ism'. They wrote with a fine gush of instinct and, sensitively. They believed staunchly in their personal philosophies and were proud of their 'nativism', not blind however to the follies and foibles of their society. Surely an original and invigorating body of work had come to permanently stay in the Indian poetic scene.

This then in my opinion has given rise to what I would describe as a second classification of 'Indianness' in Indian poetry in English for aren't the so-called Indian sub-cultures subsumed by a standardized Indian 'Culture'? The word culture has wide connotations and an exposition on it strictly speaking does not fall under the purview of this essay. But the focal point of discussion here is that all these poets were in love with the traditional and cultural moorings of their societies. They hearkened to the past, to its nostalgic calls: they were romantics and idealists in sharp contrast to the modernism and neo-modernism of current literary trends. They shunned cliches: preferring to use candidly the prisetiness of the English language; they were truly neophytes in the art of writing poetry, not forgetting at the same time the classical and allusory touch.

This kind of 'Indianness' fraught with local and regional sentiments did not fail to touch the literacy sensibilities of the rest of the country and these poets were immediately recognized for staking poetic claims and voices of their very own. They were propelled by their own poetic conscience and genius, intuitively feeling the urge to write what has already been termed as 'ethnic' poetry.

Yet what were the actual social themes in their poetry? A careful analysis reveals that there is in their poetry a deep seated conflict between 'what is' and 'what could have been' the hiatus as it were between past and present. This is turn created a poetic tension and tinged their poems with a metaphorical sadness. There is no apparent lamenting in their poetry but there are wounds; wounds which can only be healed with the passage of time or perhaps even not. A strong historical sense pervades the best of their poetry capturing moments of reality and the dialectical dichotomy between reality and realism. A lot of their verse is rich for its song like utterance of tired revellers and sunburnt time-weary myths and passions. How do we recreate the past?, is their ontological but tired question. The elements of hurt, tiredness, sadness recur as motifs in their poetry: impelling, wraithlike and haunting.

The dialogue between the urban and the rural thematically weaves into their poems and much of them is dialogic and dialectic in this best sense between the inner contemplated realities and the outside world. At the same time the modern *angst* of being and becoming besets their poetry layered as it is with deep humanistic perspectives, with the 'rural' or 'small town' syndrome.

This is a theoretical construct or framework that I have attempted to build to analyse their poetry in broad terms. A very positive element in it is a finely tuned introspection and the ability to achieve moments of self criticism. I will now take up individual poems for study and relate some of them atleast to the broad theoretical assumptions cited above.

Desmond L. Kharmawphlang looks at the past in an ambivalent manner writing of it at times, with a kind of ferocity. The historicity is permeating, yet the past and the present interface with the sense of longing; the emotional pause created between the past and the present leads to sadness layered with irony; notwithstanding a touch of sarcasm. Let me quote the poem in full:

> "I never get tired of talking about my
> hometown,
> In sumer the sky is pregnant,
> Swollen with unborn rain.
> Winter arrives, with a tepid sun
> touching the frozen hills, the dream
> boats on lakes.
>
> Long ago, the men went beyond the
> Surma
> to trade, to bring home women
> to nurture their seed.
> Later came the British
> With gifts of bullets, blood-money
> and religion.
> A steady conquest to the sound of
> guns began.

Quite suddenly, the British left,
There was peace, the sweet
Smell of wet leaves again.
But in the wavering walk of time
there came those from the sweltering
plains,
from everywhere.

You stricken Land, how they love
Your teeming soil, your bruised children,
One of them told me, "You know,
Yours is a truly metropolitan city"

(*Khasia in Gwalia* pg. 22)

Similarly in his "The September Song" and Robin. S. Nnangom's "The Strange Affair of Robin. S. Ngangom" there are vibrant portrayals of the current society and of social trends experiencing painful, horrific processes of change and transition. The poets here voice an anguish yet there is objective distancing from the subjective reality when the poet finds solace in the self:

". . . My love, how can I explain
that I abominate laws
which punish a man for his past,
only the night seems to understand
that we must bear it again.

When I am gone
I would leave you these:
a life without mirrors,
the blue ode between pines
and the winter sky, the
secret understanding of
roots and the earth,

But where can one run from the homeland,
Where can I flee from your love?
They have become pursuing prisons
which hold the man
with criminal words."

("The Strange Affair of Robin. S. Ngangom;
*Khasia in Gwalia* Pg. 38)

Like Desmond, Almond Dean Syiem too has a strong historical sense with almost a kind of euphoria. If Desmond Kharmawphlang's is "the conquest" Almond's is "the Welsh conquest", the Welsh connection in the Khasi Hills, the advent of the Welsh in Shillong in the nineteenth century, saw a new alphabet and a new religion: Christianity. Such an historical awareness recreated imaginatively brings to mind the historian E.H. Carr's question — "what is history"? Almond. D. Syiem says brusquely:

". . . A pale face, god sent young man
entered once our mistwoven hills,
brought us letters, literature and the Bible.
He was a Welshman.

The Tommies, however, brought spite
spattered the fern with our fathers' blood
and spoke to us in gunfire tones"

(*Khasia in Gwalia*, Pg 9)

Kynpham Singh Nongkynrih writes about the Earth Summit, a cosmic event in an ironical, trenchant vein. The poem is satirical and is a caustic comment on politicians yet it is intertwined subtly with the humanizing touch, tempered as it were with sadness:

"The first ever Earth Summit
was given a big build-up for weeks,
almost like the death of Rajiv Gandhi.

. . . At Nan Polok
the parking lot
humbles down
fifteen of our proudest
Pines"

("The Parking Lot"; *Khasia in Gwalia* Pg 54)

His "Winter Song" vivifies the charming winter season in Shillong and is once again an intrusion into the social fabric of the times; of what is 'happening' around us:

". . . The nights cavort with willing virgins
and virgin drinkers, singing hymns
in wobbly tones."

(*Khasia in Gwalia* Pg. 56)

It is pertinent to observe here that Desmond Kharmawphlang, Almond Syiem and Kympham Nongkynrih are also effectively bilingual poets writing felicitously both in English and their mother tongue Khasi. Poetry after all knows no language, is god-inspired, resonating with the music of words. These lines of Almond Syiem point to such universality:

"There's something about the wind tonight,
something I cannot explain.

. . . There's a man walking across the sky.
There's a river running across the
universe.

There's something descending upon us,
Something like rain, something like
the flood of tears and joy.
. . . Send me a delegation of angels,
send me a word of love,
and I'll tell you of bleeding roses,
of poems written by the fireside
of mornings drunk with your face"

The lines are quoted from his poem "Something Going On".

The discussion under consideration here has not taken into account a group of women poets in their mid twenties and thirties. The omission has been made not because of the question of quality but because of the fact that I have attempted to mainly highlight the commonalties and the shared poetic ideals of the poets illustrated above. The women poets also area an inseparable part of the Shillong Poetry Society and one of them Anjum Hasan has to be read for her powerful lines, depth and clarity. She has been published in major poetry journals of the country including Sahitya Akademi's prestigious "Indian Literature".

The dexterous intermingling of social, political, historical, satirical and personal themes make these Shillong poets a class apart by themselves. These are the canons of poetry by which we are to study them critically. The paper has only been able to give to the reader a taste and sampling of their poetry. I hope I may be forgiven for this.

# 11

# Contemporary North-East India: Problems and Prospects

*Wasbir Hussain*

Fifty years after India's independence, the country's north eastern frontier continues to be known to the outside world as a land of rugged beauty and constant turmoil. The region comprising seven states, encompassing an area of 2,55,000 square kilometres and inhabited by more than 30 million people, is best known as one of the hottest insurgency theatres in Southeast Asia rather than for its rich and vibrant culture, virgin forests, exotic wildlife, vast crude oil and mineral resources or even its luxuriant tea production.

For the first two decades since Independence, Indian leaders kept themselves busy in addressing broader economic concerns, giving shape to the country's foreign policy and grappling with the nitty-gritty's of administering the nation. The North-East did not figure high on New Delhi's agenda during this period except, perhaps, the realisation that this was a strategic area that needed concentration of military strength. This led to an impression that the Indian leadership actually regarded the North-East as a buffer against possible foreign aggression and hardly anything more.

The gradual development that was taking place in the country did not have any trickle-down effect in this region that continued to remain as the backwaters of India. This bred militancy and a strong sub-national fervour among sections of people in the north-east who started viewing the Indian rulers as a bunch of exploiters.

By the mid-sixties, militancy had come to strike roots in the region and gave rise to dangerous-looking insurgency movements with separatist designs. The North-East was soon to get caught in the vicious cycle of the lack of development and meaningful opportunities giving rise to insurgency and the violent means of the insurgents ultimately retarding development and economic progress whatsoever.

The partition of India caused a part of the then mother state of Assam to merge with the newly created state of Pakistan, resulting in the vital transportation links between the north-east and the rest of India being severed. The region was left with more than 4,500 kilometres of external frontier, connected with the Indian mainland by a narrow 22 kilometre corridor through Siliguri in West Bengal which has come to be called the Chicken's Neck. For all these years, the very considerable market disruption, socio-economic distancing and the retardation that resulted have neither been adequately appreciated nor compensated for by the Indian government.

The result of this lack of concern has been that the mindset of a substantially large section of people in the region is anti-Delhi or even anti-India. This continues to be so despite the money being pumped into the area by the centre, often without any accountability worth the name or consideration of factors such as the capacity to absorb. Today, despite the lack of industrialisation, the Net State Domestic Product in the north-east is growing at the rate of 11.2 per cent per annum at $4.29 billion, indicating a relatively high purchasing power of the people here compared to the rest of the country. Fire-fighting measures as pumping money has not solved matters and militancy continues to be on the rise.

The mood of the people in the North-East varies from anger to frustration. Things have come to such a pass that significant days in the national calendar have come to carry no meaning among the masses. Occasions such as Independence Day or Republic Day have come to be reduced to a mere governmental affair with people showing hardly any enthusiasm to associate themselves with them. The separatist guerrilla groups on their part have made it a point over the years to give calls to boycott these functions and, thereby, register their protest and highlight their demands. In this 50th year of independence, however, the government of India seems to have recognised the unique problems of the North-East. It has also come to be accepted that a rapid development in a planned manner with location-specific projects holds the key for a possible solution to such basic problems as unemployment that in turn can effectively douse the fire of insurgency if not bring them to an end.

For this, credit to a great extent goes to the United Front Prime Minister H.D. Deve Gowda who had demonstrated that breaking set norms and a flexible approach can touch even the hearts of die-hard rebels. Gowda began by spending six days at a stretch in the north-east, touring the states and getting to know first-hand its peculiar problems. He succeeded in striking a chord among the people of the region.

Gowda announced a Rs. 6,100 crore exclusive economic package for the north-east in October 1996. What is important here is a government's gesture borne out of a clear understanding of the ground reality and not whether the package simply comprised ongoing projects or whether it was left unimplemented.

The focus on development aside, Gowda's catchword was peace. He broke protocol by agreeing to personally meet the leaders of the banned Isac-Muivah faction of the National Socialist Council of Nagaland at Zurich in February 1997 during one of his stopovers there. He not only became the first Indian Prime Minister to have held direct talks with a group of Naga rebel leaders in three decades but succeeded in achieving a breakthorough. The Gowda-NSCN talks in Zurich can indeed be called a breakthrough because that eventually led to the ceasefire between the two sides effective August 1, 1997 and then formal negotiations for an acceptable solution to the 50-year-long Naga insurrection.

Prime Minister Gowda followed up these efforts by setting up a high-level committee on infrastructure development in the North-East. This committee went on to recommend a whopping Rs. 28,000 crore to give the region its basic minimum services and adequate infrastructure for possible industrialisation. The fact that an amount as high as Rs. 28,000 crore was recommended for a sector such as infrastructure in itself indicates the magnitude of the gap in the region's development sector that has widened over the years.

Some vital statistics, which I would like to back-up with the enclosed charts, goes to reveal that the north-east has been stagnating for the past five decades with an extremely tardy economic growth:

- Proposed industrial investment in the seven North Eastern states between August 1991 to December 1994, under the post-liberalisation economy, was a mere Rs. 2,224 crore (of this, Rs. 1,038 crore was for Assam). In states like Maharashtra, this figure, during the corresponding period, stood at Rs. 67,978 crore; in Gujarat Rs. 59,709; and in other equally underdeveloped states like Orissa, it was to the tune of Rs. 3,085 crore (Chart 1).
- Proposed employment as a result of these investments during the period mentioned above was projected at 5.81 lakh in Maharashtra, 4.49 lakh in Gujarat, 42,804 in Orissa and a mere 6,907 in the whole of the north-east (Chart 2).
- State-wise approvals of foreign direct investments between August 1991 to June 1995 was Rs. 7,214 crore in Maharashtra, Rs. 3,701 crore in West Bengal, Rs. 1,744 crore in Orissa, Rs. 91 crore in a small state like Goa while in the north-east, it was less than Rs. 13 crore (Chart 3).
- Only 16 letter-of-intents were actually signed for projects in the north-east between 1991 to 1994 whereas Maharashtra signed 450 of them, Gujarat 372, West Bengal 55, Goa 33 and Orissa 24 (Chart 4).
- Even the growth of the small-scale sector is not satisfactory in the north-east. As on December 1993, only 33,098 SSI units were registered in the north-east while in Uttar Pradesh, the figure stood at 2.68 lakh, in Madhya Pradesh 2.20 lakh, West Bengal 1.43 lakh, and Orissa alone 17,257 (Chart 5).
- The performance of Employment Exchanges in the north-east during a specific year 1995 shows that here had been less than 1 per cent placement out of the live registers that record more than 18 lakh unemployed youths in the region that year (Chart 6).

**CHART: 1. Statewise Industrial Entrepreneurial Memorandum Period: 1-8-91 to 31-12-94**

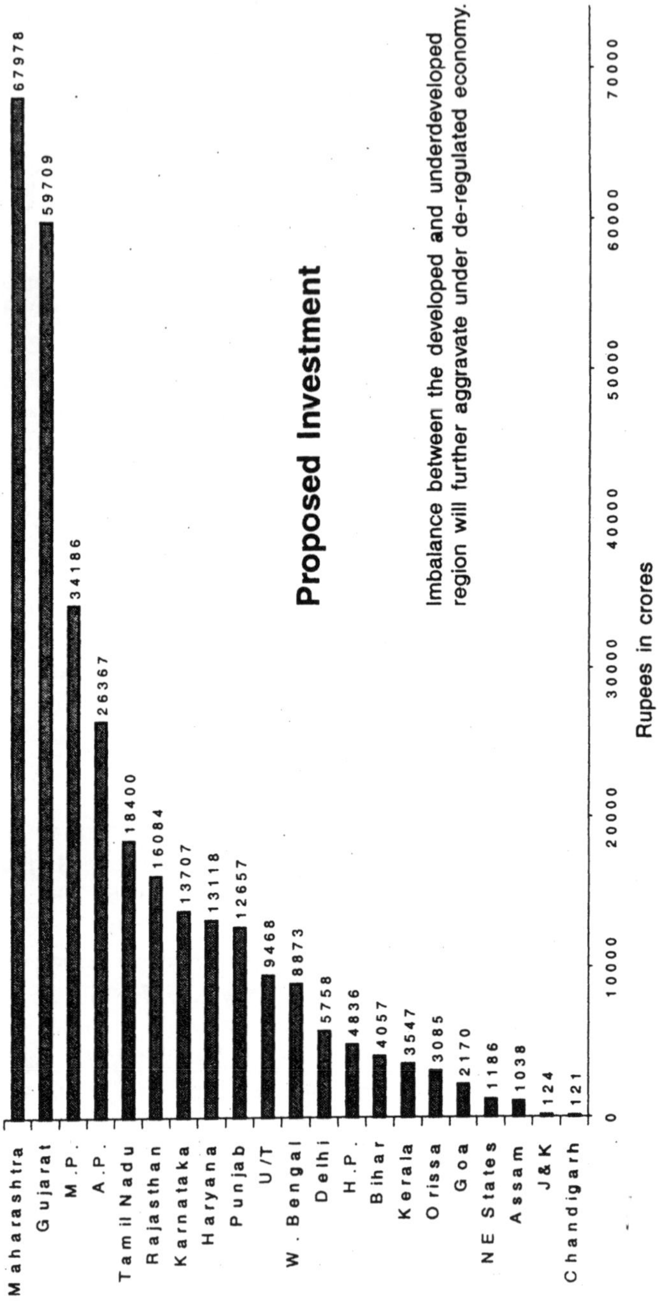


Source: Dept. of Industrial Development, Ministry of Industry

CHART: 2. Statewise Industrial Entrepreneurial Memorandum
Period: 1-8-91 to 31-12-94 (Proposed Employment)

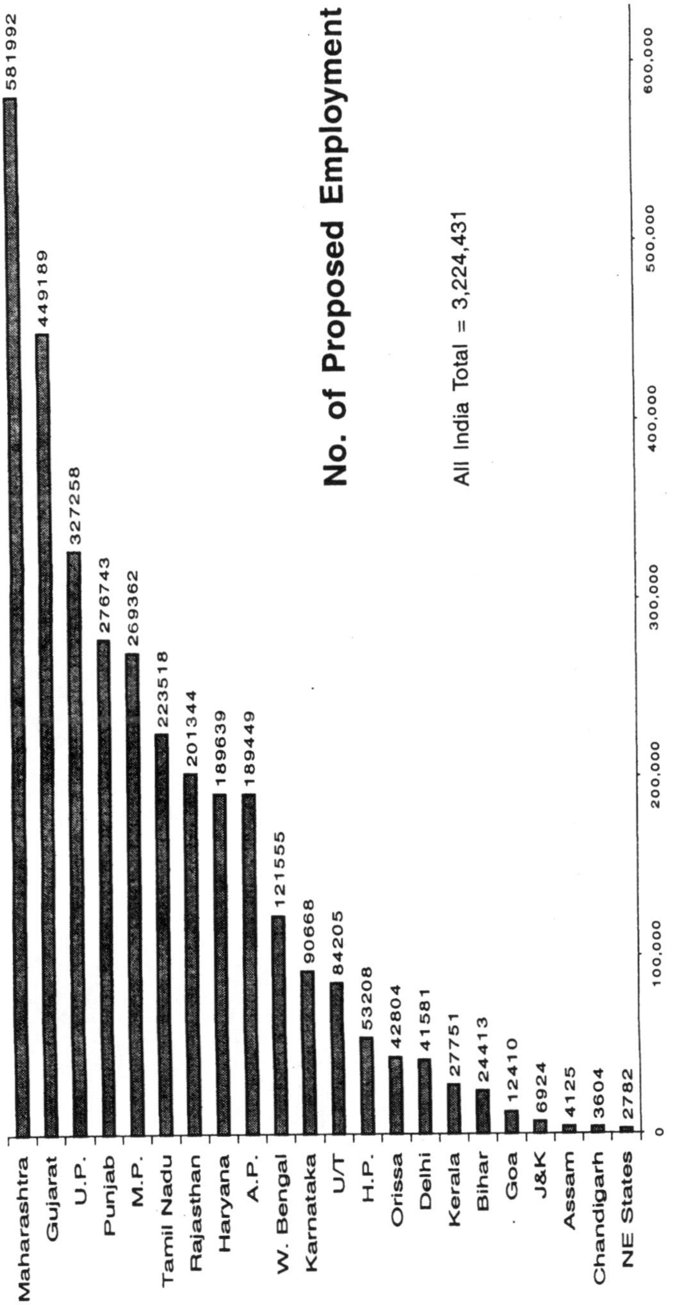


Source: Dept. of Industrial Development, Ministry of Industry

CHART 3. Statewise Approvals of Foreign Direct Investments (August 1991 to June 1995)

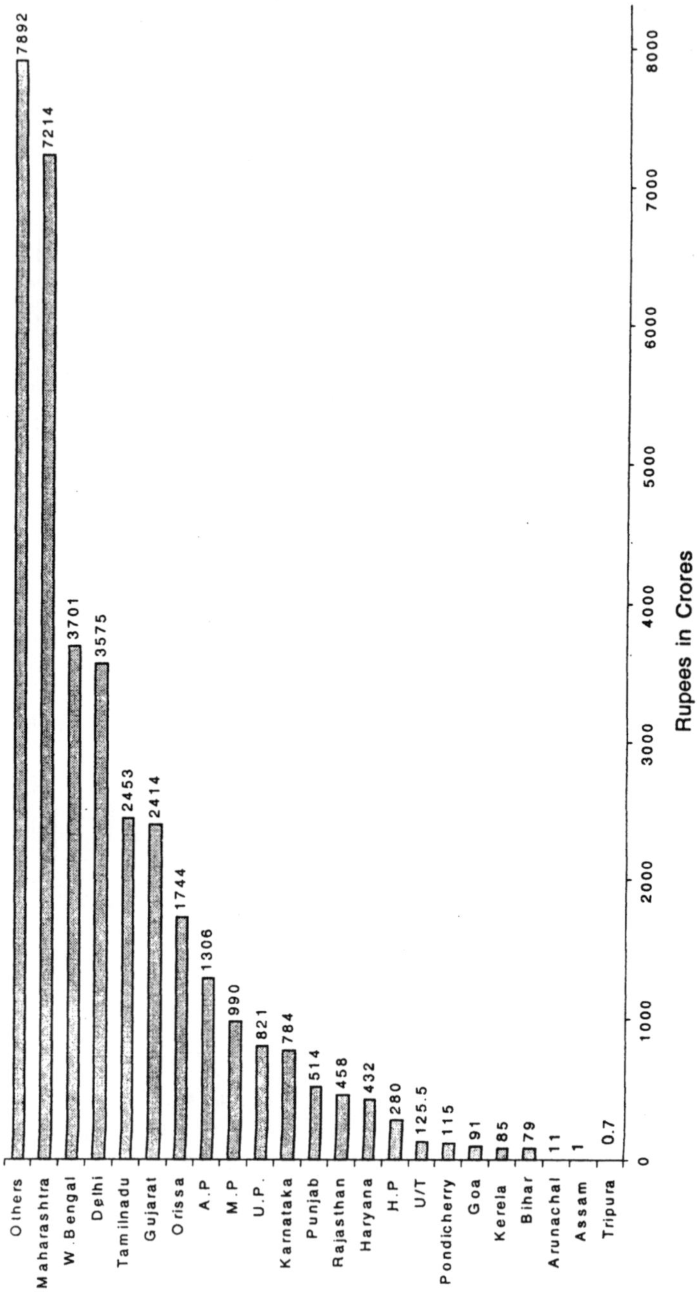


Source: CMIE: Balance of Payments, July 1996.

**CHART 4. Statewise Break-up of LOI (for the period from 1991 to 1994)**

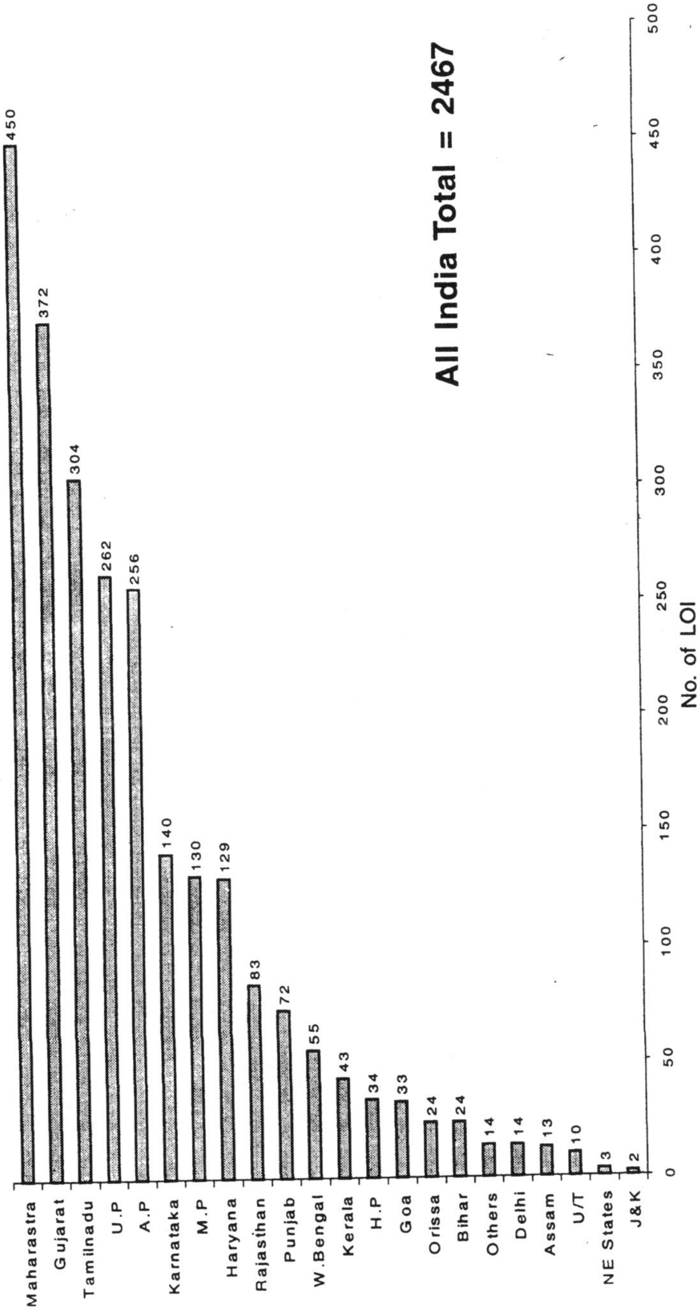


Source: Dept. of Industrial Development, Ministry of Industries

**CHART 5. Statewise SSI Units registered as on 31-12-93**

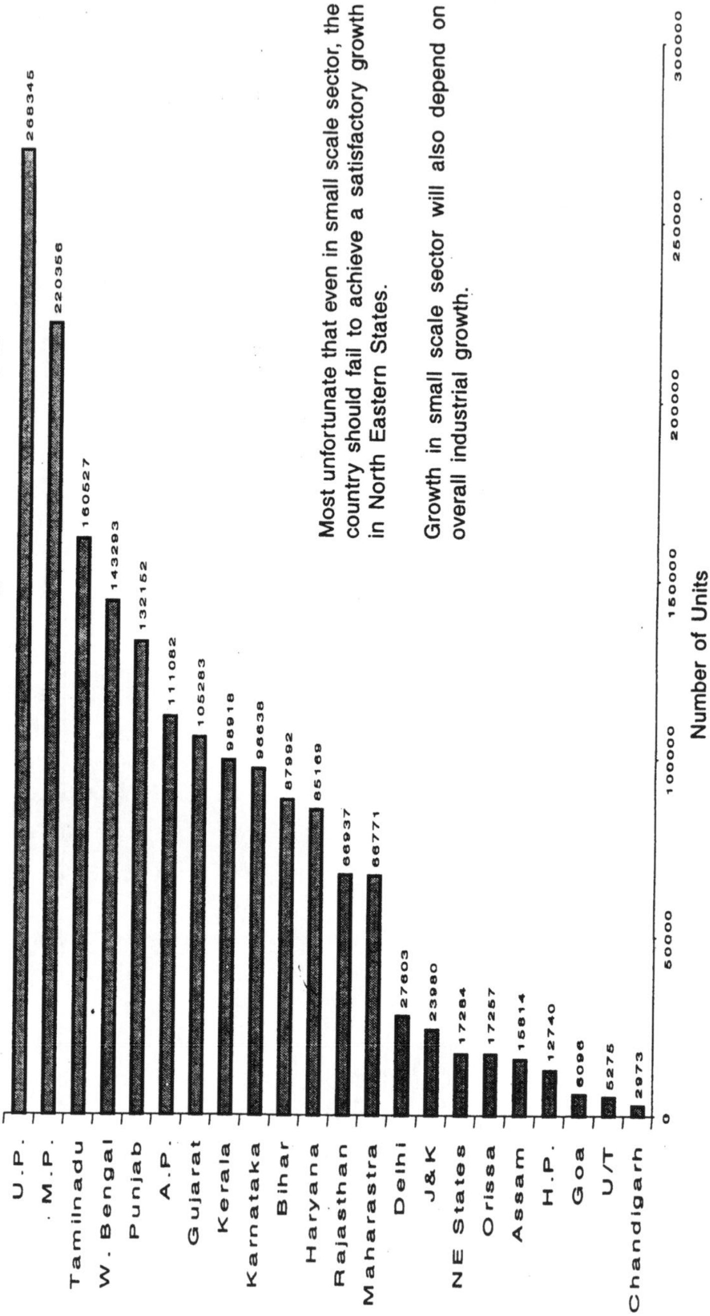


Most unfortunate that even in small scale sector, the country should fail to achieve a satisfactory growth in North Eastern States.

Growth in small scale sector will also depend on overall industrial growth.

Source: Dept. of Company Affairs, Ministry of Law

**Chart 6. Performance of Employment Exchanges during the year 1995**

| 1 | 2 | 3 | 4 | 5 | 6 | 7 |
|---|---|---|---|---|---|---|
| State | Registrations i.e. Additions | Vacancies Notified | Placements | Live Register December 1995 | % of placement on yearly addition i.e. column 2 | % of placement on live Register i.e. column 5 |
| Assam | 18,800 | 7,300 | 2,500 | 1,246,800 | 13.29 | 0.20 |
| Manipur | 29,900 | 500 | 100 | 268,800 | 0.53 | 0.37 |
| Meghalaya | 8,400 | 800 | 200 | 27,600 | 1.06 | 0.72 |
| Mizoram | 9,300 | 1,800 | 200 | 45,700 | 1.06 | 0.43 |
| Nagaland | 500 | 400 | 100 | 20,700 | 0.53 | 0.48 |
| Tripura | 17,900 | 800 | 300 | 204,600 | 1.59 | 0.14 |
| Arunachal Pradesh | 2,300 | 100 | NA | 8,400 | NIL | NIL |

Source: National Employment Services

With less than 1% of placement out of Live register of Employment Exchange, possible repurcussions should be obvious.

• State-wise assistance disbursed by all financial institutions cumulative upto March 1993 was only Rs. 972 crore for the north-east while this figure for Maharashtra was Rs. 23,068 crore, West Bengal Rs. 5,018 crore, Orissa Rs. 2,635 crore and Goa Rs. 810 crore (Chart 7).

Statistics cannot always be dismissed as lied, specifically when figures as the ones I have quoted above have been compiled by agencies of the Government of India. These statistics goes on to show a stagnant economic condition resulting in: increasing unemployment, perceived feeling of being neglected and frustration among the youths, manifesting itself in various forms including militancy.

The saddest part of this state of affairs in the north-east is that its underdevelopment is not the least caused by the lack of resources or potential. Coopers and Lybrand, a consultancy firm of international repute, had come up with a very optimistic report in 1995 on the vast untapped potential in the North-East that could turn this region as a key player in India's possible role as an Asian economic Tiger.

The report noted that the North-East has a strong base for mainstream as well as downstream industries with a plethora of mineral resources (oil, natural gas, coal, lime-stone, mica, granite etc.), a wide range of roast-based crops and agro-based plantations, vast investment potential in the infrastructure sector and one of the most fertile stretches of land along the Brahmaputra, fit for commercial cultivation.

In fact, Coopers and Lybrand's projection of the North-East, due to its locational advantages, as the gateway to some of the fastest growing economic centres of Southeast Asia like China. Thailand, Myanmar, Malaysia or the Philippines has triggered of a new ray of hope for the people as well as planners in India. Suddenly, it seemed possible that the north eastern region which is connected to the Indian mainland by the narrow Siliguri corridor can be better connected to the Southeast Asian market with an estimated 200 million households.

The World Bank, too, enthused the optimists to a great extent by trying to forge ahead with its South Asia Regional Development Initiative. This initiative includes the north-east as a key player along with Bangladesh, Bhutan, Nepal and the

**CHART 7. Statewise Assistance Disbursed by all Financial Institutions Cumulative upto March 1993**

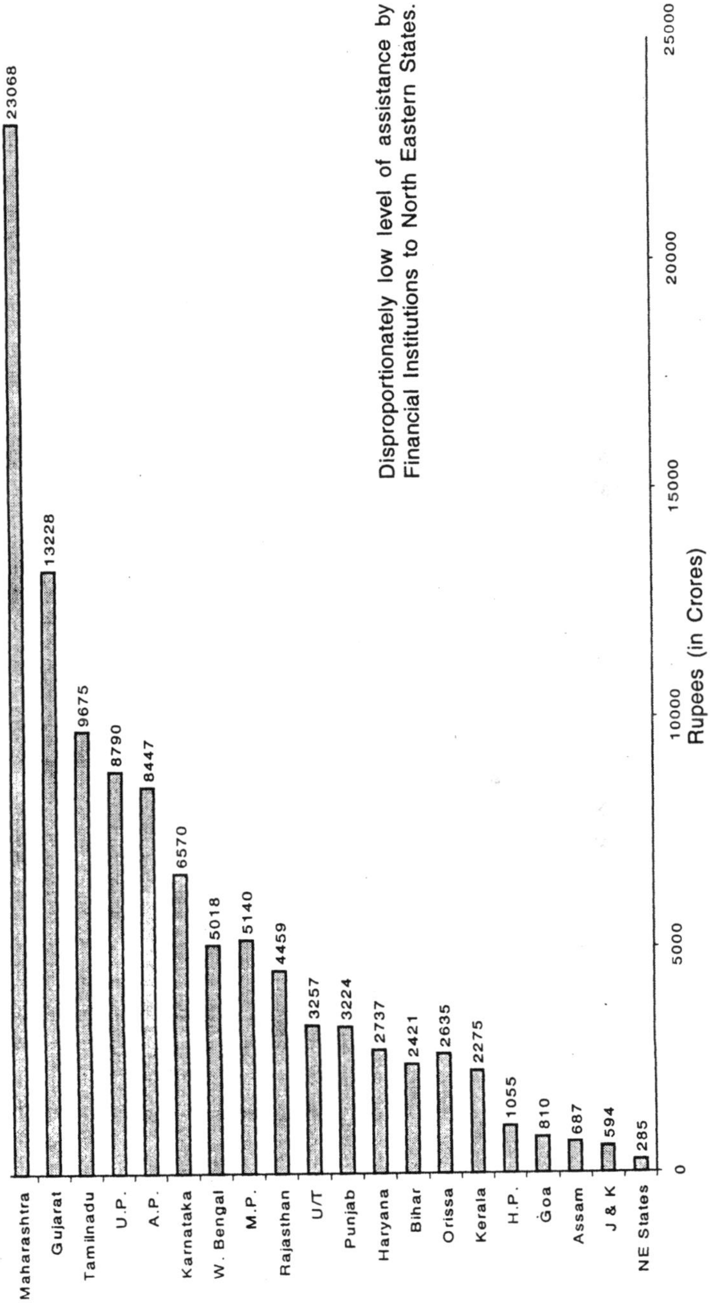


Source: Department of Company Affairs, Ministry of Law

eastern Indian states of West Bengal, Bihar and Orissa. Another body that sees this region as a potentially big economic player is the Indo-US Joint Business Council which had *The Emerging East* as its theme during its meeting at Calcutta in December 1997.

If these dreams can be translated into reality we can have things happening in the north-east like transboundary road and rail links, access to ports through joint port development, water transport like development of inland waterways and coastal links besides energy trade in the gas and hydro power sectors.

To make even the slightest headway in this great project north-east, the private sector has to play a very big role. But the private sector's concerns are many, which include: lack of government commitment, limited paying capacity of consumers, political instability and civil unrest, poor policies and inadequate legal and regulatory frameworks, limited institutional capacity/experience with project financing and lack of credit worthiness of sub-sovereign governments (state governments)/public off-takers.

Besides, the private investors are shy of investing in the North-East due to its geographical isolation, inadequate communication, poor infrastructure, lack of market within the region and higher cost of setting up projects. The conversion cost in the region is high due to prolonged rainy season and heavy rainfall leading to less effective working time per year for construction and other disadvantages associated with industrially backward regions.

Taking into account these factors, a report by the Engineers' India Limited shows that the gestation period of a project in the North-East is 5 years against 4 years for a similar project elsewhere, cost of site work and erection contract is 25 per cent higher and civil and structural cost is 15 per cent higher.

Therefore, the government has to step in by way of providing incentives. This has happened, of late, with the centre coming up with an exclusive industrial policy for the north-east.

But, subsidies or incentives alone cannot work wonders. What is required in the north-east today is a dedicated set of political entrepreneurs who consider the state or the region above everything else. What we need are statesmen with a vision and a commitment to get rid of the rut that has set in this region and not just a bunch of professional politicians. Corruption at high places must be reduced to a minimum if not eliminated and a consensus approach in planning required.

Towards the objective of ushering in meaningful development, the student groups in the North-East and the militants, too, can contribute their bit. The student organisations in each of the North-Eastern states wield considerable influence. But so far, they are only channelising their energies on political issues. They don't have a clear-cut or well-defined economic agenda for their respective states.

One can expect wonders if these powerful student groups keep aside their differences with the State Governments in so far as handling of state-specific issues are concerned and cooperate on a programme exclusively concerning development.

On their part, the rebel groups, too, cannot shirk responsibility towards the region's economic growth. Even while carrying on with their bush-war against the Indian state with a view to realising their political demands, the separatist guerrillas need to see reason and should not obstruct the development efforts if not extend cooperation in taking them further.

After all, the rebels agitating for different forms of self-determination must realise that economic growth and development are permanent things which are going to remain in the areas and the people for whose well-being they are supposed to be fighting for. Only some sort of a social revolution can succeed in driving home this point to these sections of our society.

All is not lost yet and there is certainly hope for the north-east. But to usher in a possible golden millennium, the seven states must work in unison and with one voice so as to make distant Delhi appreciate and keep the region high on its agenda. Agencies like the North Eastern Council must wake up from its slumber, get rid of its gross inefficiency and try to take some pride in fulfilling its role as an apex development planning agency for the region. Else, there should be a public as well as governmental outcry in the whole region against such an agency.

New Delhi can also try and demonstrate its sincerity towards the region by accepting the widely recommended proposal for setting up a separate ministry for north eastern affairs in the union government.

In the end, what is required is the need for a change in the mindset of the people in this region. Xenophobic feelings would not take us anywhere. If we can come up with rational views and ideas, if we can have a set of honest and dedicated politicians with a vision who are sincerely backed by the people and if Delhi genuinely supports the develop north-east scheme, we can indeed have a different story to tell about this far-eastern Indian frontier.

# 12

# The Trend in Journalism in India's Northeast

*Sanat K. Chakraborty*

**"The contact of Assam with the rest of the world began with the publication of *Arunodoi* 150 years ago by the American Baptist Missionaries, and it was through this journal that the renaissance of Assamese language too had first begun. . ."— Syed Abdul Malik.**

This writer attempts to briefly outline a few important aspects that set the trend in print journalism in the northeast region during the last five decades.

Newspapers talk of people and their works, as many other academic disciplines; they mirror societies and their social, economic, political, cultural and even psychological dynamics that trigger off change. Though print journalism was ushered in the region with the publication of the first newspaper, *Arunodoi*, by an American Baptist missionary Fr. Nathan Born in 1846 from Sibsagar, upper Assam, the launching of *The Assam Tribune* as the first English daily was very significant.

"Since the publication of the first newspaper, *Oroonudoi* . . .", wrote *The Assam Tribune* in its golden jubilee publication in 1989, "a few newspapers in English and Assamese were brought out by enthusiastic men with a view to promoting the interests of the province, but they were short lived." Therefore, it further said that "there was an acute need for an English newspaper . . . to articulate the needs of Assam in particular and to rouse the people in this part of the country in the struggle for independence in general. This meant that Assam was badly in need of an English newspaper with nationalist outlook. . . ." Of course, there was an English weekly, *The Times of Assam*, published from Dibrugarh in upper Assam, which generally served the interests of the tea plantation community.

It was clear that *The Assam Tribune* appeared exactly 100 years after the publication of *Arunodoi* in the context of Indian freedom movement and the political uncertainty of the Assam province in the wake of the partition and other political events. The out break of the Second World War, the Quit India Movement, the British Cabinet Mission Plan, the Partition of Indian subcontinent, emergence of new nations and the Communist take over in China led by Mao Tse Tung, added new geopolitical and strategic dimensions to the frontier areas. To a great extent, the newspaper succeeded in articulating the interests of the people in Assam and moulding public opinion. The choice of English as the *lingua franca* was equally important as the newspaper tried to reach out to all sections of people — plains folks and hill tribes. It was the only daily newspaper read all over the region, and in a way, representing the interests of composite Assam.

Of course, many saw *The Assam Tribune* primarily articulating the majority Assamese interests, such as, its strong opposition to the British Cabinet mission grouping scheme of dovetailing Assam with Bengal; its stand on Sylhet referendum, influx of refugees from East Pakistan, thereby warning the then political leadership of "disastrous effect on Assam's future — politically, culturally and in other vital spheres" (*The Assam Tribune* Golden Jubilee [1939–89] publication).

On the one hand, the newspaper strongly advocated the integration of the Assam province into the Indian Union, and on the other, vehemently opposed the merger of the province with Bengal. It was obvious that the Assamese leadership wanted to get rid of the Bengali hegemony and secure self rule for themselves within the Indian federal framework. While the Assamese leadership led by late premier Gopinath Bordoloi retained the provincial autonomy and politico-administrative control, the assertion of Assamese rule and its stand on the future of Sylhet somehow alienated the Bengalis, the second largest population in Assam. Some even suggest that the launching of *The Shillong Times*, from Shillong, the then capital of Assam by a Bengali in 1947 should be seen against these political developments.

During 1947–71 a discerning reader may see an uneasiness in the newspapers in articulating people's interest or defining issues, as the region was undergoing drastic politico-administrative changes. The composite Assam began to crumble. So was the contours of 'Assamese interests', as the state grappled with sweeping political problems: the Naga separatist struggle, the Mizo uprising, the anti-Assamese language movement by hill tribes of Assam. The creation of Nagaland in 1962 and the re-organisation of the northeastern region in 1970, were bitterly resented by the Assamese leadership and hoi-polloi alike and this was reflected in the newspapers in the state. This political assertion by the Assamese leadership gave rise to identity questions as various ethnic communities began to express that feeling through autonomy demands or even hill state movements. The result: the fragmentation of polity, and the splintering of the media vision.

Beside this, there were unexpected external political developments too, such as, the invasion of Tibet (1959), the Chinese aggression of India (1962), the Indo-Pak war (1965) and the liberation of Bangladesh (1971), which overwhelmed the people of northeast frontier states and confounded the situation. The people of Assam also experienced the vulnerability of the Indian union and the helplessness of the central government to deal with national crises and their eventual fall out. It was a psychological blow, from which the region has never really recovered. "One of the serious handicaps from which this state has suffered in its relation with the Centre is comparative ignorance in Delhi of the nature and complexity of Assam's problems", *The Assam Tribune* stated in its editorial on April 2, 1965, on the Silver Jubilee anniversary and claimed that "to fight this ignorance has been a guiding objective of this newspaper."

**Growth of newspapers in a fragmented polity:** in search of space for expression.

During the last five decades, particularly the post-reorganisation period (1970–90), we also witnessed a sea change in the societies of diverse communities and cultures in the vast valleys and hill areas. Moreover, the spread of education and growing political awareness along ethnic lines gave impetus for creating space to define socio-economic and political issues and concerns of various communities. In last 50 years many English and language newspapers and periodicals appeared, of which only two dailies — *The Assam Tribune* and *The Shillong Times*—could see their golden jubilee years. A good number of newspapers wilted away within less than a decade, but at the same time, some others made new appearances. And now, not less than 250 dailies, weeklies and other periodicals are hitting the news stands at different places in the region. In Assam alone, there are over 20 English and language dailies and more weeklies published from different parts of the state. In Meghalaya, we see at least two English dailies published from Shillong only. At least one English daily and a half dozen language newspapers are published in each of the seven northeastern states. Mizoram has even scores of locality newspapers cyclostyled giving a summing up of the village or locality news.

Unlike other parts of the country where media developed itself into a major industry, newspapers in the northeast continued to act as a platform of expression. And in the process, the newspapers, because of their massive influence on public opinion, became a powerful tool of social change, and in some cases even ethnic assertion.

In the context of infrastructural and financial handicap as is present in the NE, one would wonder how do all these newspapers survive? The most important requirement for the survival of a newspaper is advertisement support. Generally, industries contribute the main revenue through advertisement to the newspapers. In the northeast, however, except for the gradual expansion of government departments and development programmes, there is hardly any economic activity; the region is industry-starved. Secondly, the readership of almost all the newspapers is area-centric which does not go beyond their place of publication. Even the dailies like, *The Assam Tribune, The Sentinel, The Eastern Clarion*, among a few English dailies of Assam with relatively popular standing have no significant presence in other sister states.

So we see a very unique situation: on the one hand there is limited circulation and near-zero private advertisement support and on the other, mushroom growth of newspapers. How is it happening? One answer is government support through official advertisements. And another answer is the support of vested interests. We have already indicated how the entire polity got fragmented on ethnic lines and how this affected the development of media in the region. Some people think that newspaper can wield power by moulding public opinion, and that urge for power is a big factor that motivate people to launch newspapers; secondly, some seek to come to lime light via media and finally, many think one can make a lot of money through publishing newspapers. Therefore, to some, it is not really important whether a newspaper is economically viable or not. Rather it has become a forum for self-expression, as no newspaper could any longer ensure space for all sections of people living in the region. Therefore, we have *Arunachal Times* for Arunachalis, *Bodoland Times* for Bodos, *Tripura Times* for Tripura, *The Nagaland Post* for Nagaland, *Free Imphal Press* for Manipur so on and so forth.

Of course, one may argue that despite the growth of media in isolation, there is an attempt to redefine a new regional perspective. With the fragmentation of Assam and creation of new states, many felt that newspapers in Assam could no longer represent the interests of the entire region. Even the *The Assam Tribune* which pioneered journalism in the region, began lose its emotional appeal, whatever little it had in other parts of the region. And therefore, we could see some interesting newspaper titles — *The Northeast Times, The Northeast Observer, The Northeast Daily* and so on — appeared since early 1990s, which are trying to represent a new regional perspective.

**The handicapped local press:** Unfortunately, they do not seem to have been able to articulate the new idea as yet and remain essentially state newspapers. There are a few important factors that stiffled most of the newspapers in the region. Firstly, none of the newspapers has made real investment in developing professional skills. Since the returns on the investment made on human resource development are realised on the long term basis, there are few who are ready to wait. Most of them seek short-term benefit and therefore, put their money in opening business offices in metros, neglecting the development of basic infrastructure, that is required for producing a quality newspaper. There is very little scope of acquiring professional skills here as the newspapers fail either to train local talent or attract and retain professionals for a long time. Secondly, the lack of work culture, which is closely linked with the first problem. Most of the employees, both journalists and non-journalists, are underpaid and work with undignified terms. Most of their jobs depend on the pleasure of their employers and the former do not have space for redressal. In fact, newspaper houses discourage employees' union and harass its members and force them to quit the job when it suits them. Barring one or two newspaper houses, leave alone implementing wage board recommendations, most of them do not even issue proper appointment letters or contracts to their journalists. And finally, the communication bottlenecks which restricted the circulation of daily newspapers all over the region. The newspapers do not find it either useful, or economically viable to field correspondents across the region when they cannot use their reports on a daily basis.

*The role of metro-newspapers as a channel of objective information*: I wish to touch upon yet another perspective related to so called mainstream media — I would prefer to call them big, widely-circulated newspapers — by raising a question. What kind of information emanates from this region and finds place in these big metro dailies? A causal study of five metropolitan daily newspapers over a fortnight would reveal that only two areas were constantly focused: insurgency and insecurity. Sometimes it's about militants, at another time, it's killing or an ambush. The mainland newspapers often looked at this region, just like the rulers in Delhi did, as a perennially disturbed area and therefore, the focus of these newspapers constantly remained fixed either on Indian security concerns or on militant activities launched by various ethnic groups in the frontier states. Insecurity and killings are certainly a great concern, but how do the people cope with such a situation? These big newspapers do not have much space and time to figure out that.

The big, influential newspapers which have both the means and capacity, lack purpose and interest to research the issues and concerns of the region and bring them to the national consciousness. For them, this region is economically non-viable and posting correspondents in all the states is considered a drain on their resources. Of late, the Calcutta-based newspapers, particularly the influential *The Telegraph* and *The Asian Age* have embarked on a unique packaged journalism with catchy pull outs like, *The NorthEast Telegraph* and *The Northeast Age*, respectively. Their *modus operandi* is like this: They have found out that there is no regional daily which can reach out to all the northeastern states because of the lack of transport and communication facilities within the region. So it would make smart business sense if an exclusive news package pooled in from these states can be fed back to the landlocked and information-starved people. So we have these northeast pages exclusively for the region flown to various state capitals by air from Calcutta or Delhi which hit the news stands well before the regional dailies can reach. These newspapers could do a great job if the real issues and concerns of the region were conveyed across the country. They still can do. There is a lot of ignorance in Indian mainland about the people and happenings in the sensitive border states of the region. The mainland newspapers have immensely contributed to this ignorance and misgivings about the people inhabiting the region.

And finally, the role of media in conflict situation. Media must play a special role in the northeast, beyond its professional obligations and business compulsions: as a missionary aiming at conflict resolution.

One may argue why only talk about northeastern states? Other Indian states can also argue on the same line. Yes, they can rightly say this, but it has to be kept in mind that India's northeast has certain special historical, cultural and strategic characteristics. The region is straddled by at least four foreign countries — Bhutan, Tibetan China, Myanmar and Bangladesh and are ravaged by violent armed activities.

Therefore, in the context of India's northeast, research on media where people's aspirations are reflected, assumes great significance. How does for example, media work in a conflict situation? Can the newspapers write objectively? Do they take sides deliberately or under pressure? What kind of pressures it had to face, and then go about playing its role of seeking truth and bringing it before the people?

Recently, a section of press in Assam has been accused of promoting the separatist cause of a banned militant outfit. The state government came down heavily on a particular newspaper organisation and its editor for publishing reports that is allegedly detrimental to the maintenance of public order. The situation triggered off a public debate whether the press should have an unbridled freedom of expression that brings disorder and chaos in society. Last September, former Assam chief secretary V.S Jafa, outlining the state government's perception of the role of the press, observed: "the government and media engage in a daily, intimate interaction and at the same time, regularly accuse each other of heinous offenses. Conflict between the official right to secrecy and the press's right to publish is waged in no man's land, while the Parliament shies away from legislative clarity, and court rulings continue to leave areas of uncertainty."

He argued, as many others would, that unless one could prove that "there are circumstances under which free and critical press will help sustain national consensus and rally the nation in support of national goals, then no argument for a free press will save it in practice. No nation will indefinitely tolerate a freedom of the press that serves to divide the country and to open the floodgates of destructive criticism against the freely elected government that leads it."

In the context of North-East, the role of the newspapers has become very critical. The question is how to develop a code of ethics for professional journalists, while ensuring free flow of information or freedom of expression. The newspapers in Nagaland often complain of "double squeeze" between the threat of militants and the state government. There are many such issues which require understanding in a conflict situation.

# 13

# Trends in Healthcare in Northeast India, 1947–1997

*H. Ghonglah*

It is not an easy task to delineate the directions through which healthcare or healthscience in this region run during the last fifty years. It would also be a folly to say that we can study these trends without focusing on what took place before 1947. After all, modern medical science is hardly one hundred years old and none would deny that it came to our soil via the very British rulers whom we love to hate. Thirdly, we Indians love to pontificate on our rich 'culture' and this culture is deeply woven around our belief systems, our health practices and even our poverty. All these make this task even more difficult since as most scientists now realize, healthcare is not simply doctors and stethoscopes, it is indeed, all those things that contribute towards a healthy lifestyle.

Let us therefore go straight to what happened before 1947.

## *A Highly Decentralised Health System*

During those days the whole Northeastern region was under composite Assam and the administrative machinery of the region encompassed even Sylhet district in today's Bangladesh. The population of the region was less than half of what it is today. As far as health matters are concerned there was a Health and Sanitary Commissioner responsible for the overall health policy and implementation here. He himself belonged to the Indian

Medical Service cadre. In turn, he received help and guidance from an Inspector General of Hospitals and a Director of Public Health. All of them were highly qualified in their respective areas of expertise. What I want to emphasise here is the fact that even a white colonial ruler from across the seas, realized at that time the importance of decentralisation of power. All the policy matters about healthcare in the region were taken in the region itself. There was no need for them to run to Delhi or Calcutta for advice every time there is a cholera or Kalaazar epidemic in the region. They had all the human resources they need here.

### *An integrative, yet Clear demarcation between Curative and Preventive*

As mentioned earlier, the Commissioner worked under the guidance of an Inspector General of Hospitals and the Director of Public Health. These were the two arms of healthcare during those decades — the curative and the preventive aspect respectively. The IGH looked after the curative centres like hospitals and dispensaries throughout the region whereas the DPH was responsible for health education, sanitation, urban health planning, the fight against epidemics and even legislations for Public Health issues. We should remember that the Public Health Act was passed in England only in 1872, very close to the years when the East India Company entered this region. They must be still acutely aware of the importance of the preventive aspects of health like clean water, clean air, sanitation, nutrition etc.

Another important fact abut this system then was that there was no clash of interests between the two aspects of health and they could effectively managed at a time when the region was in the grip of serious infectious diseases like cholera, smallpox, kalaazar and so on. There were more public health legislations passed and enacted before 1947 than during the next fifty years after Independence.

### *Importance of Health Research*

As opposed to the folk remedies of the region and the Unani practices in the rest of India, modern health care cannot function effectively without research, laboratory studies and the work carried on by the team called paramedicals. Before 1947 the Assam Scientific Research Society and the Indian Tea Association were the two bodies instrumental in moving for the establishment of the Pasteur Institute in Shillong, a premiere centre then for local research on health problems of the region. There was a Ross Malaria Institute here though before 1912 the only cases of malaria in Shillong were the imported ones. There was a Public Health Laboratory where regular tests of water, food, milk consumed by the public was tested to avoid adulteration and toxins. In 1923 a list of more than 100 medicinal and economic plants of Assam was sent to the exhibition at Wembley. In other words, before 1947, health research was alive here in the region. Even the cultivation of cinchona trees producing antimalarial quinine was initiated then here.

*Serving the Interest of the Rulers*

Inspite of all these achievements, the pre-1947 health service in the region suffered a serious drawback. Perhaps it could have been corrected in the long run, one cannot say. But it was quite obvious that it was basically centred around the headquarters, that is Shillong. During those days the rest of the Northeast including Kohima, Aizawl etc. were small hamlets. So there was no health infrastructure worth the name in those places. There was a lot of debate to set up the Pasteur Institute in Haflong initially but it lost because it was thought to be 'unhealthy'. One begins to wonder whether it would not have been wiser to set up a health research institute in a place where there are more germs! Even the Cantonment areas in Shillong (and the other hill stations) were initially established to isolate the rulers from the disease and germs of the natives.

Before closing this paragraph on the pre-1947 health system in the region, I would like to remind you that there were two types of white men in our midst then. While the rulers of the East India Company had little time for the rural masses, majority of both health education work and institutes of curative health were established by the white missionaries. The first dispensary in Mawphlang in 1878, the Robert Hospital in

Jaiaw in 1922, followed by the Jowai Hospital, and a number of such hospitals and schools throughout the region both by the Protestant and Catholic missionaries was indeed the real healthcare movement in these hills. Therefore, inspite of all the other achievements mentioned earlier, the pre-1947 healthcare in the region could not continue itself effectively into the post Independence period, due to many factors as we shall see

## The Post 1947 Scene

### *Based on a Sound Theoretical Foundation*

It was as early as June 1946 that the Interim Government accepted the Bhore Committee recommendations as far as the health policy foundations of the Independent India were concerned. Provision of health services to the entire population was adopted as one of the Directive Principles of state policy of the Constitution of independent India. Health planning was rightly made an integral part of the over all planning for socioeconomic development. The planners of the first health policy of independent India realized the need to tackle unemployment, malnutrition, housing, sanitation along with the development of an integrated health service for the entire population as the prime requisite of attainment of health. Even in matters of health care, it was expected that a referral by any Medical Officer from any dispensary in the country will be duly accepted by the premiere medical Institution like the All India Institute of Medical Sciences in Delhi.

### *A Highly Centralised System*

Inspite of the fact that health is a state subject, events in post 1947 Northeast India showed that it is being remote controlled from the Centre. When the British rulers left, the IMS cadre also left, bringing in their generalist counterparts in the form of the IAS and the region was left virtually without any health thinkers. A number of vertical programmes especially like the Family Planning Schemes, the National Malaria Eradication Programme, the Small Pox Eradication Programmes took over the time and money of most states and they become mere 'mechanics' of a health care system which was highly controlled from above. Even the budget for health and education, two pillars of any growth in a society never crossed beyond 3 percent throughout the years.

### *Preventive Health Slowly Disappeared*

When there are no state health planners of repute, and when the region becomes a mere laboratory for the curative specialists of Karol Bagh or Connaught Place, this naturally leads to the slow death of all that we understand about preventive health. It was in 1950 that the then Govt. of Assam took away water supply from the health department and created the separate PHE department for the mere reason that it has become too 'big'. Quantity has now become a more important reason for change of policy rather than quality. The earlier role of the inspector General of Hospitals and the Director of Public Health are now looked after by one overall Director of Health Services. And in states like Meghalaya, today, there is no role for the Director of Public Health. His place instead is taken over by the Joint Director of Malaria, of MCH or similar services. Vertical programmes initiated from the Centre have virtually taken over in the states of the region. While our cities are expanding there is no urban health department to look after environment, sanitation, nutrition, pollution and so on. Healthcare has become synonymous with curative medicine.

No doubt, the growth and development of medical colleges and big hospitals in various parts of the region after independence is a noteworthy landmark. But again here, there is a note of caution — all these institutes can at best produce good 'medical mechanics' not health planners and educators as the Bhore Committee initially anticipated.

### *Health Research Non-existent*

It is a shame to say it but it is true that within a short span of fifty years, there is no health research worth the name in the whole region. The region that once had the Assam Scientific Research Society and the world renowned Pasteur Institute,today,is known more for the antics of an eccentric 'pig-heart' specialist rather than revolutions in epidemiological and health research related to the day to day life of the people. Where are studies to show the relationship of bad water supply to the gastroenteritis and similar maladies of the people? Where are studies to show us the per capita consumption of liquor by our men when we talk so much about the destruction by alcoholic drinks in our society? Healthcare without health research is quackery at best. The Public Health Lab and Malarial Institutes are no more and the Pasteur Institute simply exists in name.

### *Healthcare for the Rich*

All the egalitarian concepts enunciated in the Bhore Committee report today, are being mutilated in the health service system prevailing in the country and the region itself. It is one thing for the white colonial rulers to keep themselves aloof from the flies and the mosquitoes of the natives. But it is even worse when the rulers of Independent India used the same machinery 'bequeathed' to them by the colonial rulers to perpetuate their hold on the government of the day and to keep their fellow Indians below the level of human dignity. Today, in the whole Northeast India, take any sample survey and one would find that those who go to health centres and government hospitals are the poorest of the poor. They go there not because it is good or better but because they cannot afford to go elsewhere. Of course, there are exceptions but these are extremely rare. If one wants a better quality healthcare one would have to be rich, first or to know how to steal without getting caught!

Earlier, we mentioned about the first national health policy where a patient referred by any government doctor from any part of the country will get preferential treatment even in the highest centres of medicine in the land. But today after fifty years, unless one is related to the VIPs of the land, that chit from your doctor is worth a toilet paper. That's what we mean by the healthcare that caters to the rich and the powerful rather than those who really require its services most.

*Neither Here nor There*

At least in other parts of the country, they may lack in basic preventive health but their curative health services are exceptionally good. But today in the Northeast we are still far behind the rest of the country even in our curative healthcare. That's what I mean when I say that we are neither here nor there. And this will continue to remain so until and unless we develop a political will and resolve to change things. To immediately embark on a programme to produce the needed human resources who have a vision, and who are willing to work as a team. Because health is not merely absence of disease. It is a lifestyle, a culture and a virtual way of life.

## BIBLIOGRAPHY

1. D. Banerji. Health and Family Planning Services in India.
2. S.R. Mehta. 1982. Sociology of Health and Medical Care.
3. S.K. Sahu. 1980. Health Culture of Oraons.
4. T. Singh. 1978. Health care at community level.
5. H. Ghonglah. 1996. Strong medicine Weak System.
6. H. Ghonglah. 1996. The Church and Healthcare in the Northeast.).
7. K.W. Newell. 1988. Selective Primary Healthcare.